PRAISE FO.

"If your lead gen needs a Red Bull, Tom's book is here."

- ANN HANDLEY, Chief Content Officer of MarketingProfs and *Wall Street Journal* bestselling author

"If you want extreme results, you can't rely on common practices. Tom walks you through bold and innovative ways to transform your lead generation results. The book will help you rethink your strategy and push you to achieve far more for your business."

- JEFF COYLE, Co-founder and Chief Strategy Officer, MarketMuse

"This is a must-read book for folks that want to inject more creativity and lateral thinking into their lead generation efforts. If your lead generation strategy is stuck in the ditch, *Rethink Lead Generation* is a tow truck to get you back out on the freeway."

- APRIL DUNFORD, Author of *Obviously Awesome*

"If you think lead generation is a formulaic application of marketing tactics (essentially a numbers game) this book should expand your vision of how much more can be achieved with imaginative thinking and coordinated creative execution across channels. The right marketing can become an engine for generating customer advocacy and unpaid distribution. THAT is the formula to apply - and Tom knows how!"

- SARAH FAY, Managing Director, Glasswing Ventures

"Being in the business of helping brands leverage content to tell authentic stories that engage people and build relationships, I strongly encourage you to read Tom Shapiro's *Rethink Lead Generation*. It will not only open your eyes to the power of creativity and lateral thinking in content marketing but will also deliver a firehose of ideas for you to explore in achieving greater leads growth."

- ANDREW WHEELER, CEO, Skyword

"If leads are the lifeblood of your organization, you need to read *Rethink Lead Generation*. The 'best practices' you are trying to follow may be ineffective or even harmful. Shapiro offers a fresh take on how to get leads, even in highly competitive environments."

- ROGER DOOLEY, Author of *Friction* and *Brainfluence*

"Being more innovative than the competition really pays off. I've experienced it firsthand. Tom Shapiro shows you how creative approaches to organic lead generation can ignite impressive results. His enthusiasm is contagious, and his endless flow of ideas is energizing."

- GABI ZIJDERVELD , CMO, Smart Eye

"Packed with eye-opening, yet actionable advice, *Rethink Lead Generation* shows you exactly how to transform your lead generation approach to get the results you need today. Read it and you'll feel like Tom is right in the room with you, passionately guiding you to idea after idea that will drive your lead growth to new heights."

- NANCY HARHUT, Chief Creative Officer, HBT Marketing

"Get ready for greater growth. If you're looking for a new way to think about lead generation, a 'rethink' if you will, then you will really enjoy *Rethink Lead Generation*. Tom additionally provides thoughtful insight to how content marketing and SEO provide real fuel to your lead gen engine."

- KENNETH KINNEY, host of "A Shark's Perspective" marketing podcast

"I worked with Tom for more than six years as his team managed our network of 45 websites and saw firsthand how deeply he thinks about driving leads growth. We continually brainstormed new ways to capture more leads, and with his help our company grew exponentially over that time."

- VIJI DAVIS, Principle, IRI

RETHINK LEAD GENERATION

ADVANCED STRATEGIES TO GENERATE MORE
LEADS FOR YOUR BUSINESS

TOM SHAPIRO

Copyright © 2022 by Tom Shapiro

All rights reserved.

No part of this book may be reproduced in any form or by any electronic or mechanical means, including information storage and retrieval systems, without written permission from the author, except for the use of brief quotations in a book review.

Published by Stratabeat, Inc.

https://stratabeat.com/

Cover design by Mike Krupsky

ISBN 978-0-9991847-4-5 (paperback)

ISBN 978-0-9991847-2-1 (hardcover)

ISBN 978-0-9991847-1-4 (ebook)

Additional Resources:

RethinkLeadGeneration.com (Book Website)

TomShapiro.com (Author Website)

Stratabeat.com (Marketing Agency Website)

❦ Created with Vellum

CONTENTS

Introduction	ix
1. Lateral Thinking And Creativity	1
2. Transforming Your Website Into An Unstoppable Leads Engine	32
3. SEO and Content Marketing	76
4. Account-Based Marketing	148
5. Referrals	175
Conclusion	190
Notes	191
About the Author	195
About Rethink Your Marketing	197
Book Tom To Speak At Your Event	199
About Stratabeat	201

INTRODUCTION

One idea. Six-hundred and fifty pieces of content and a $23 million pipeline.

Is it marketing fantasy? Or is it truly possible for a business-to-business (B2B) marketer to achieve this type of content marketing success?

The marketing team at SAP was trying to address 25 industry verticals (healthcare, airlines, telecommunications, etc.) in their marketing when they faced this dilemma. Historically, they would have selected three to five of the most relevant verticals, created customized content for each, and then called it a day.

When planning to build content on the topic of digital transformation, however, they realized the topic was just as relevant to one vertical as to all the others. There was no way to select merely three to five. They felt it was their responsibility to figure out how to get the content into everyone's hands across the 25 verticals.

"Just about every firm with which we've spoken over the past five or more years is focused on transforming their business,"

SAP's Global Content Lead, Ginger Shimp, explained to me. "There's a deep sense of urgency to innovate, stay current, stay relevant, stay competitive. In fact, were you to Google 'digital transformation', you'd likely break the internet!," she joked.

Shimp continued, "Strategic leaders today understand that failure to focus on the high-impact strategies that are shaping the firms of tomorrow will result in getting left behind. Therefore, in order to reach both our current customers as well as our net new prospects, we set out to create a thought leadership campaign to help executives develop a deeper understanding of these trends affecting the future of business through fact-based executive research, supplemented by the latest thinking from executive peers and industry experts, and packaged in a consumable, conversational format. From there, we branched into a comprehensive demand generation campaign driven almost entirely via digital outlets."

SAP not only rethought the way they were creating content to serve multiple verticals, but also rethought the very notion of content scalability itself.

Where to start?

The team at SAP started with a single whitepaper. They then turned to templatizing that whitepaper to enable the creation of vertical-specific versions, bringing in industry experts in the process. The idea was to create a base product that would be 80 percent the same across verticals and then fully customize the remaining 20 percent for each individual industry.

How to scale beyond vertical-specific content?

Beyond the industry-specific segmentation approach, SAP also rethought the format of the whitepaper. The theme at SAP was to slice and dice the content and then slice and dice and slice and dice it some more.

Instead of a standard whitepaper, SAP produced a suite of content. The team took the industry-specific whitepapers, extracted key information, and created the following derivative content for each industry:

- 10-20 blog posts
- 2 infographics
- 5 tweet cards
- 1 podcast
- 1 video whitepaper
- Multiple "how to" and "customer testimonial" videos
- 1 audiogram
- 1 webinar
- 1 pitch deck to explain SAP's Digital Transformation story
- 1 "TED Talk" video
- 1 one-page summary doc
- 1 whiteboard to train the sales team on how to pitch the pitch
- 1 value survey to see where people were in their digital journey

On top of this, SAP's team customized the content for the following audience segments:

- Technical Users (advisors)
- Middle Management (influencers)
- Executives (decision makers)

Standardizing the process across industries helped to achieve the economies of scale needed to support 25 verticals. One piece of content was used to promote another, all acting in concert to drive greater engagement.

All of this content was housed in unique, industry-specific digital hubs. It was an all-out atomization of the content by what Shimp coined a "Digital Chop Shop™" within SAP, and it's a powerful method for scaling one's content marketing. Put it all together, and SAP generated 650 pieces of customized, snackable, digitally native, socially shareable content as part of the campaign. This content ecosystem was ready to work hard as a lead generation platform.

Since this original campaign, Shimp has gone on to replicate the method with numerous other campaigns, adding increasingly new variations such as audio whitepapers and narrative podcasts to expand reach into newer audiences.

Did the 650 pieces of content produce results?

In spades! Within a year the initiative resulted in more than:

- 96,000+ blog views
- 26,600,000+ social media impressions
- 43,708 unique contacts from 14,200+ different companies
- 15,300 social engagements
- 21 percent cross-industry share of voice (SOV)
- 21,700+ TED video views
- 16,124 radio listeners

On top of this, there were thousands of infographic views, blog referrals, whitepaper downloads, new prospect inquiries, and qualified leads.

Most impressively, the campaign generated $23,488,300 in pipeline.

Get Unstuck

If you're unable to achieve the breakthrough marketing success that SAP's Shimp and team demonstrated with the Digital Chop Shop, if you're exhausted trying to get your B2B marketing to work, or if you're stuck on a plateau from which your team cannot escape, this book is for you.

Rethink Lead Generation explores strategies, channels, and methods for you to cut through all the noise, break free from ineffective marketing, and enrapture your audience. The book goes beyond strategies to gain attention and helps you guide your audience to the actions that matter most.

If you're frustrated that your current lead generation strategies just aren't cutting it, you need to rethink what you're doing. Continuing what you've been doing in the past isn't going to get you to the next level. Tinkering around the edges doesn't unleash growth. Copying competitors doesn't work. And chasing after the latest media obsession won't help you either.

What you need is a new framework built on creativity and lateral thinking. Seeing the non-obvious. Doing what might seem impossible (or even crazy) to others.

Lead Gen Websites To SEO To Behavioral Intelligence

Rethink Lead Generation covers a variety of lead generation strategies, approaches, and tactics. The book walks you through dozens of ways to grow your leads organically. SAP's Digital Chop Shop approach to content marketing is just one in a series of powerful examples that can help spark new ideas for your brand. From lead gen websites to search engine optimization (SEO), content marketing, IP detection, conversion optimization, behavioral intelligence, account-based marketing (ABM), and referrals, you'll walk away with new, actionable insights.

What the book doesn't cover is paid media-based lead generation. In my experience, organic lead gen delivers a far higher ROI over the long term. With paid advertising, you are essentially renting your audience. You pay for each click. As soon as you stop spending on ads, your traffic drops to zero. With organic approaches, you're earning your audience's trust and you're building relationships. The results compound over time. For any business that wants to win longer-term, organic lead generation is the more effective and sustainable approach.

There's no one cookie-cutter method for organic lead generation, and *Rethink Lead Generation* will help you explore various options so you can determine the most effective strategies for your particular brand.

Rethink Lead Generation includes first-hand interviews with innovative marketing leaders, including trailblazers such as Ginger Shimp at SAP, and others at Drift, Tableau Software, WP Engine, and many more. In addition, this book is filled with many case studies of rethinking in action.

Throw out the best practices. Use marketing jujitsu. Get ready to challenge your current approach and rethink your lead generation strategies.

Enjoy the book, enjoy the lead generation ideas, and enjoy the many leads you'll be generating after reading the book.

1
LATERAL THINKING AND CREATIVITY

When you think of expanding reach at the top of the funnel, you might think of strategic partnerships or you might think of advertising. Or, perhaps you might think of SEO or direct mail.

Would you think of ruining the Facebook IPO?

That's exactly what Larry Kim, founder of WordStream and MobileMonkey, did, on his way to over 10,000 press mentions within a week.

Three days before the Facebook IPO while still at WordStream, Kim published an article and infographic on the WordStream blog with the results of a research study he had conducted comparing the effectiveness of Google Display Network and Facebook ads.

The research was based on criteria that included advertising reach, ad targeting options, advertising performance, and supported ad formats. His conclusion was that Google was a far better option.

"Everyone was very excited about the Facebook IPO, very bullish, and I was the only marketer in the world to publish a negative study that compared the ad performance of Google ads versus Facebook ads," Kim explained to me. "I gave a very unfavorable rating to Facebook. And of course, because this was contrary to what everyone else thought, and because it was very timely, because every freaking newspaper organization on the planet was writing about this IPO, it actually ended up getting picked up with over 10,000 media placements."

Kim's team timed the launch of the article for 9am Eastern Time on May 15, three days before the Facebook IPO. They pumped out a press release and asked friends in the industry to help bring attention to the article. By lunchtime, organizations such as Business Insider, The Wall Street Journal, and MediaPost had written about the research. By the afternoon, The Wall Street Journal announced that GM was dumping all of its advertising on Facebook, citing the WordStream research as a possible explanation. This then got picked up by ABC, CBS, The Washington Post, USA Today, CNN, Fast Company, The Economist, Mashable, PCMag, and others.

That same day, they started getting phone inquiries from TV and radio stations, ranging from the BBC to NPR.

The WordStream crew was quick to adapt to the news narrative. The article was originally titled, "New Research Compares Facebook Advertising to Google Display Network: Who Comes Out on Top?" When the GM story broke, though, they released a similar press release with a slightly different title: "Does Facebook Advertising Work?" Because the news media were scrambling to identify reasons for GM's dramatic move to stop all Facebook advertising, it only made sense to redirect the focus of the content.

Capitalizing on the momentum, Kim wrote follow-up pieces, including "Why I Dumped My Facebook IPO Shares at the Open Today," to keep the media coverage going strong.

Kim and other executives wound up being interviewed about the research by hundreds of media outlets, including BBC News, CNN, and The Associated Press. Overall, Kim estimated that more than 10 million people around the world had either read or heard about the story.

Ensuring this wasn't a one-hit wonder, his team published at least one big story quarterly. But if you ask Kim where marketing is going in the future, he immediately responds that you need to think laterally and do something different. Doing the same thing as you did in the past usually doesn't make a difference.

"What I do is come up with something really weird instead," Kim told me. "Some blogs, they're patting themselves on the back when they get a 20 percent increase in leads in a year.

"My goals were a little bit more ambitious, trying to achieve some kind of geometric increase." Kim explained. "Doubling every seven or eight months, or something like that. All I can tell you is that the future of lead generation is definitely not going to be any of the channels you've heard of. Or maybe it could be one of the channels you've heard of, but not in the way that you're currently using it. And by the time I tell you what it is, it's too late.

"You kind of have to have this really creative mind, this growth hack-y, marketing scientist mind to ideate crazy ideas and execute on them," Kim continued.

One of the growth hacks that Kim employed early on with MobileMonkey, for example, was partner webinars. In doing partner webinar after partner webinar (14-15 webinars monthly), Kim was able to build a massive email opt-in list within a mere six months. I'm not at liberty to share the specific number of opt-ins with you, but let's just say that many B2B companies probably don't build a list that large even after six YEARS.

Ladies and gentlemen, you now know the power of lateral thinking and creativity in marketing.

The Best Business Ideas Are Often the Most Laughable

Reid Hoffman was one of the co-founders of PayPal, and then went on to co-found LinkedIn. He was Executive Vice President of PayPal when it was sold for $1.5 billion to eBay. He's now a Partner at the venture capital firm Greylock Partners, and his net worth is in the billions. That's a resume that's hard to top.

As with the case of Larry Kim's Facebook research, Hoffman understands that it sometimes takes deviation to unleash growth, even if those ideas make others laugh out loud.

According to Hoffman, it's sometimes the best business ideas that are the most laughable at first glance. "The lesson for entrepreneurs," he stated on his podcast *Masters of Scale*, "goes deeper than the pat advice that you shouldn't take 'no' for an answer. You should expect to take 'no' for an answer. If you're laughed out of the room, it might actually be a good sign. Google, Facebook, LinkedIn, and Airbnb all sounded crazy before they scaled spectacularly."[1]

Being contrarian is not only valuable, it's critical. It's how many breakthrough ideas are formed. And how breakthrough results are achieved.

Hoffman continued, "The first truth of entrepreneurship and investing is that the very big ideas are contrarian, because the contrarian is part of the reason why a bunch of large companies and competitors haven't already done it, why a bunch of other entrepreneurs haven't already succeeded at it.

"And so that leaves space for the creation of something — and to create something big, you have to have that initial space. For example, in the early stages of Google, search was a terrible way of making money in advertising, because advertising is time-on-site. And what does search do? It shuffles you off the site as fast as you can go. That's not a good business model. So at Airbnb, someone's going to rent a couch or a room from someone else? Who are the freaks on both sides of that transaction? So all of these things have this kind of similar quality — very smart people will tell you, there's no there, there."

Being Crazy Is Often The Route To Crazy Good Results

Hoffman points to the importance of lateral thinking in business concepts. It's just as powerful when it comes to cutting through the noise, attracting an avalanche of attention, and driving massive revenue growth.

Want to build a company that exceeds $21 billion in annual revenue? Meet Salesforce.

Think it followed a typical course on its journey of acquiring new customers? Think again.

When Salesforce was founded, Siebel Systems was the 800-pound gorilla in the customer relationship management (CRM) software market. Siebel Systems software cost hundreds of thousands of dollars, including long-term professional services contracts. The software was complex and took years before it was clear if your organization would achieve ROI with the platform. Everyone at the time simply thought that it just had to be this way. It had to be this unpredictable. It had to be this painful.

Contrast this to Salesforce, which offered a cloud-based software, available to use the same day that you signed up. All for $50 a month with a credit card, where you could cancel at any time.

Marc Benioff, Salesforce's founder, realized that the company couldn't go head-to-head against Siebel, so instead they chose to engage in marketing jujitsu.

Soon after launching Salesforce, the company staged a protest just outside Siebel's annual user conference at the Moscone Center in San Francisco. The fake protesters chanted, "The Internet is really neat ... Software is obsolete!", in alignment with Salesforce being the first cloud-based CRM software.

As part of the protest, Salesforce staged a fake TV crew. All the activity brought so much attention that actual live TV crews started showing up. Salesforce team members approached as many people as they could who were heading into the Siebel conference and gave each one an invitation to the Salesforce.com launch party that evening.

Twenty Siebel executives called the police.

Meanwhile, more than one thousand organizations signed up for Salesforce within two weeks.

With that, Siebel would hand industry leadership over to the scrappy startup. Lateral thinking 1. Siebel 0.

Doing The Opposite

Tim Cook, Apple's CEO, was once asked by a student at his alma mater, Duke University, about whether the student should listen to his professors. Cook responded by saying that he felt one should rarely follow the rules and should instead write their own rules.[2]

That means, if your company has been doing its marketing a certain way over the years without change because that's the way it's always been done, it's time for you to shake things up and try something radically new.

At a digital marketing agency prior to my founding of Stratabeat, a colleague and I proposed something that a member of the executive team considered utterly laughable. Until, that is, he saw the results (and became a major cheerleader of the initiative).

When I had joined that agency, the firm's top marketing investment was sponsorship of large industry conferences. Each event would cost around $30,000, $40,000 or $50,000. We had a large booth at many such events, and spent hundreds of thousands of dollars annually in the process.

Thinking laterally, however, a colleague and I questioned the value of spending so much money on events where literally dozens of our competitors were fighting for attention right next to us.

Instead, we thought, what if we did the opposite?

Instead of trying to get in front of as many prospects as possible, what if we just got in front of the *right* prospects, where we controlled the environment without any competitors in the room? What if instead of five minute conversations we could engage with them in long, thoughtful discussions?

That was the genesis for hosting our first local happy hour event. We had just opened a new Chicago office, and so decided to go local and host an event there. We rented out a room filled with comfy sofas at the House of Blues in Chicago. The first event drew merely 10 attendees. We brought in a guest speaker from Google to speak about the future of search. We handed out books by Avinash Kaushik, Google's Digital Marketing Evangelist and author of the book *Web Analytics 2.0*.

It might seem insane to focus on events with one or two dozen people instead of thousands, but that's what we did.

The result?

One of the attendees at the first local event signed a seven-figure contract with us, and another a six-figure contract. Booyah!

At the next event, we landed another seven-figure client. From there, the events turned into a road show and became the number one leads driver for the agency. Whereas it had taken the company nine years to reach 85 employees (I was the 85th), in my five years there we grew to more than 700. Explosive growth by any measure.

Sometimes, you just need to experiment with the exact opposite approach to what you've been doing in order to increase your most profitable leads. (No matter who laughs at you when you propose it.)

Why Best Practices Suck

Marketers often seek best practices. It's almost comical how many times you'll hear marketers talk and write of the best practices to which they adhere.

The problem with best practices is that almost everyone starts to adopt them, and then you're merely a copycat brand in a sea of sameness. It's a one-way trip to mediocrity.

Sure, the best practices may have worked for a few companies initially, but eventually everyone and your second cousin is conducting their marketing in line with the best practices, and innovation and creativity then grind to a halt.

When a corporate buyer is looking for a solution, and they are faced with six or seven options that all look the same, sound the same, and act the same, it's difficult for any of those firms to make the sale, let alone achieve breakout growth.

Why do so many marketers adhere to best practices?

Because it's safe. No one is going to laugh or yell at them. No one is going to point a finger and call them stupid. If they fail, they can hide behind their claim of best practices, and so it feels less risky overall.

Be better than best practices. Be true to the DNA of your own brand. Know your audience better than anyone else in the industry and connect with them more deeply. Deviate from the norm. Be creative, be unique, and be true to your brand. As Tim Cook says, write your own rules.

And ditch the best practices.

Firing 50 Percent Of Clients To Unleash Growth

I started my career at Panasonic in Tokyo. In my four years at the company, I participated in an effort to constantly grow the customer base. Makes sense, right?

Well, let's contrast this with my next work experience, where I was part of another "unthinkable" initiative...growth through elimination.

I joined a Japanese translation company in the Boston area as the Sales and Marketing Manager. One of the first things I noticed about the company was how busy everyone was. The phone was ringing, and quotes were going out the door continuously. The company was servicing every type of business imaginable, running around accommodating request after request.

Then a group of us at the company realized that there was one type of client that was more valuable than all the rest. That was software companies, with massive documentation sets and online help systems that required translation and localization with every release.

When I first arrived at the firm, orders from non-software clients were as low as a few hundred dollars. A software company on the other hand, would enter agreements with us worth hundreds of thousands of dollars...per release.

It became obvious that the best way to spur growth was to focus on software companies as our target audience. That would mean, though, that we'd need to do something very counterintuitive.

We'd be required to fire 50 percent of the company's clients!

That's right. We'd need to ask literally half of our customers to go away and give their money to a competitor instead.

Yet, what happened after firing our clients was nothing short of an explosion of growth. We were finally free to focus on our best clients, and to be exceptional at what they valued the most. This, in turn, helped us to build expertise and differentiation in serving software clients, which helped us accelerate our new client close rate, with each deal exponentially larger than the average size deal when I had first joined the firm. Profitability increased dramatically.

Everyone within the organization was on the same page, and it became a smooth-running machine. In fact, we were closing business so fast that we maxed out our production capacity and started turning prospective clients away.

Once we fired half of our clients and focused instead on software companies, revenue grew by 250 percent within approximately two years.

Continuing to serve our customers while trying to attract more software clients was certainly one option at the time. It would have been the course that perhaps most companies would have taken.

However, where you will find the greatest growth is when you take bold action based on lateral thinking. Think outside the box. Think of doing the opposite of what you've done in the past. Look ahead to the future with blazingly clear vision. The unorthodox approach can set you free.

Giving It All Away

Another form of lateral thinking is to brainstorm ways to give away your product for free. That's right, just give it away. Nothing in return. No revenue. Just a bunch of nothingness. (Yes, this is another "laughable" idea.)

Yet, that's exactly the type of counterintuitive thinking that can spur massive growth.

SolarWinds Worldwide is the company behind Pingdom, a website performance monitoring solution. One of Pingdom's functions is page load time testing. The faster your web pages load, the happier your site visitors are likely going to be, and the more conversions your site will likely generate.

Pingdom has long offered a free tool for web page load time testing. The tool is completely free. You can test the time it takes for any of your web pages to load from one of various server locations around the world. Want to test multiple pages? No problem, there's no limit to how much or how often you use the tool.

Now, why in the world would the folks managing Pingdom think this was a good idea? Shouldn't they charge at least a minimal fee? Or put a cap on its usage? Or upsell you every time you use the tool?

Well, when you consider that more than 34,000 websites link to the tool, representing over 4.4 million backlinks, you can see the power of the free offer. For anyone who knows SEO 101, high-quality referring domains and backlinks are extremely important ranking factors in Google's organic search algorithm. At the time of this writing, the free testing tool page is ranking on Google page one for more than 1,000 keywords, representing 164,000 monthly U.S. Google searches. So, on top of giving prospects a chance to test out part of the functionality of the Pingdom solution, it fuels lead generation through SEO.

Elissa Fink, the former CMO of Tableau Software who helped take the firm from tech startup to public company with $1.15 billion million in annual revenue, relayed a similar tale to me. When I asked her about one of Tableau's most successful lead generation tests, she walked me through the offering of a free version of Tableau's data visualization software, and explained that traffic and usage truly exploded when they offered the free version.

No longer was the tool used only by specialists or larger companies, but was adopted by a much broader range of companies, organizations, and people.

It acted as an easier way to get prospective customers trying out, playing with, and using the software. It was an entryway for a large number of future upgrades to Tableau's paid products. On top of this, close to 100,000 websites created more than 9 million links to the free tool, again helping the company to gain countless leads through organic search.

It might seem counterintuitive, but introducing a free offering may open the floodgates for leads and future revenue.

Kickstarting Something Big

Shane Atchison, former CEO, North America at Wunderman Thompson and former CMO at Domo, told me a story that gets right to the heart of why lateral thinking and creativity (and "laughable" ideas) are so powerful in achieving breakthrough marketing results.

Atchison was CEO at an agency at the time, when an online video company approached his firm. Although the video company had achieved significant traction among younger demographics, it was having a difficult time with older males. They tasked Atchison's agency with capturing this demographic's attention.

As I was talking with Atchison, he informed me of his passion for creativity and innovation. To that end, he would huddle with his team every day in brainstorming new ideas for this client.

One day, a generally quiet team member spoke up. He mentioned that he noticed a guy named Erick Sanchez on Kickstarter who wanted Kenny Loggins to play in his living room. Sanchez needed to raise $30,000 to make it happen.

There were a number of donation levels on Kickstarter, but a fan favorite was surely the Holy Guacamole Package, which stipulated that for a $750 donation, you would be guaranteed a seat in Sanchez' living room, a t-shirt, AND a batch of his household famous guacamole for you to enjoy during the show.

Atchison's team thought about it, and then the "laughable" ideas started pouring forth. Someone in the room then suggested that they call Jimmy Kimmel and see if he'd be interested in a video call with this Kenny Loggins-loving dude during an episode of Jimmy Kimmel Live.

Jimmy bit. Game on!

They conducted the video call, garnering an outrageous amount of attention among the older male demographic for Atchison's client. Due to the appearance on Jimmy Kimmel Live, the story was captured by ABC News, The Washington Post, HuffPost, NPR, and various TV news channels.

As a result, Sanchez reached the $30,000 goal, and Kenny Loggins performed in his living room. (I hear that Loggins rocked the house.)

The moral of the story? Creativity wins!

Doing What Won't Scale

Another form of lateral thinking that's "laughable"? To focus on marketing that doesn't scale. At all.

The marketing team for the revenue acceleration platform Drift decided early on to do something that is not only not scalable, but is extremely time consuming. The team, as part of its theme of being authentic and human in all of its audience interactions, decided to reply to every single social media post, whether on Twitter, Instagram, LinkedIn, or elsewhere.

In the book *This Won't Scale*, the marketing team explains that it's a tough thing to explain to others: "You can't get in front of your board of directors and say leads were down but we replied to every tweet last month."[4]

Let's face it. Quantifying the ROI of a tweet for a B2B software platform is nearly impossible. But this is why it's so brilliant. By making sure that everyone who converses with the brand gets a real human reaction, Drift is engendering a flood of brand love.

And does focusing on things that don't scale help the business? Well, Drift is one of the fastest-growing SaaS companies ever and achieved a $1 billion valuation within six years. On top of this, they have an army of fans. I'd say that they scaled the business nicely!

Booking It

I've been working in the digital marketing world for a long time. First on the client side, and for the past 16 years on the agency side. The first website I launched was several years before Google was introduced to the world. There was no such thing as ecommerce. Yahoo existed, but was a link directory without any graphics at the time. We're talking the dinosaur era of the web.

I've been deeply enmeshed in the evolution of the digital world ever since. Whether launching new websites or executing SEO programs, whether developing digital marketing plans or conducting behavioral intelligence analysis, I have been immersed in many angles of what drives business online.

So, it might seem counterintuitive that I would think that turning to a hard copy book would be a good thing to focus on to spur further growth at our agency, Stratabeat. When having breakfast with the CEO of another firm here in Boston, he told me that a book should be the *last thing* that I spend my time on.

Yet, publishing my first book, *Rethink Your Marketing: 7 Strategies to Unleash Revenue Growth*, helped us to increase our leads and conversions substantially.

Besides leads, there were many benefits to the book. Our team has used the book as a hook to greatly expand our publicity, land speaking gigs, secure interviews, and increase our mailing list, as well.

Of course a book lends credibility to the business, but in terms of demand and lead generation, where it really became a powerful force was as a tool to be integrated with everything we were doing.

Lateral Thinking And Creativity

It opened the door to countless publicity wins that, in turn, drove many leads.

For example, the book helped us to land speaking gigs at conferences with up to 20,000 attendees. During most of these presentations, I offered the first chapter of the book to everyone in attendance, and each of these needed to opt in on a special RethinkYourMarketing.com microsite to get the chapter.

Having just published a book, I was approached by a variety of podcasts to be interviewed. This presented a fantastic opportunity to not only explain the concepts in the book but to once again offer listeners an opportunity to grab the first chapter after opting in. Some of these podcasts have subscription lists of more than 30,000, immediately enabling our message to reach a large population of marketers that would have been difficult to reach without these external platforms.

The publicity was not limited to events and podcasts either. After publication, we were able to secure a number of articles outlining certain concepts from the book in third-party publications, including Forbes, MarketingProfs.com, and ChiefMarketer.com, with a collective total monthly readership in the millions.

And of course we created offers in the Stratabeat website and the RethinkYourMarketing.com microsite for a first chapter download, further increasing our database.

On top of all the opt-ins, the conferences and interviews have resulted in a number of leads and clients.

The book has helped in closing deals, as well. When meeting for the first time with the CMO of an enterprise analytics software company with $380+ million in funding, we offered the book as a gift during the meeting. He immediately stopped us, reached into his bag, and brought out a copy of the book, exclaiming, "I already bought it. I've read the first three chapters...and I love it!" He then texted me throughout the ensuing weekend as he plowed through the rest of the book, highlighting ideas that he liked and discussing ways that they could be incorporated into his own company's marketing.

We won the deal.

Thinking laterally helped me to go beyond the limits of digital marketing when aiming to spur new growth. The book paved the way for many speaking opportunities, interviews, byline articles, mailing list subscribers, leads, and clients.

How can you go beyond the confines of your industry to create something that, although counterintuitive, may lead to significant new growth?

Understanding That Everyone Is Irrational

Everyone's irrational. Yes, I am irrational, too. So are your prospective customers.

Don't worry about it, though. It's simply a function of the human brain. Although we think that humans are purely rational and make decisions based on logic, the reality is different. And until you realize that, your marketing is bound to disappoint and underperform.

Let's take your website. Is it trying to logically explain what you offer and why the site visitor should buy it?

Here's the problem with the above scenario: You're addressing the people who visit your site rationally, explaining why they should fill out your form, download your whitepaper, sign up for your webinar, or ask for more information. Because of that

— because you're trying to reason with your audience in a rational way — you're missing out on engagement and conversion opportunities.

You may like to think your site visitors are intentional in the way they do things on your site. You may like to think they base their decisions on logic while on your site. In reality, though, even those who are the most rational by nature are driven by the subconscious.

The human brain is up to 30 times more powerful than the world's most powerful supercomputer. Check your ego, though, because almost all of that brainpower is used by the subconscious. In fact, the human brain processes 11 million bits of sensory information on a subconscious level every second.

The conscious mind? Well, it processes only about 40 to 50 bits per second. In a race, the subconscious mind would utterly smoke the conscious mind.

So how do we make decisions?

According to Gerald Zaltman, Professor Emeritus of Business Administration at Harvard Business School, 95 percent of purchase decisions are based on the subconscious.[3] How do you capitalize on that and connect with your prospects on a subconscious level? We've already seen logic is not the best way to go.

Instead, try appealing to emotion.

As humans, we are emotional creatures. The neuroscientist Antonio Damasio ran studies on people with damage to the part of the brain that triggers emotions — people who couldn't feel any emotion. They couldn't feel happy, or sad, or angry, etc.

One would think making decisions would be easier without emotional interference. But what Damasio actually found was that his subjects had an extremely difficult time making decisions, including any kind of purchase decision.

The reason? They didn't feel strongly enough about any option.

The result? Endless waffling.

Through this study, Damasio uncovered an interesting reality: humans make decisions based on emotion and only then rationalize that decision.

In other words, if your marketing is not evoking an emotional response from your audience, you're missing out on conversions, leads, discovery meetings, new customers, and sales.

This is why one person is willing to pay $50,000 for a Rolex watch, even though they could have saved $48K or $49K buying a TAG Heuer instead. It's why one person is willing to pay $100,000 for a Maserati, whereas they could have spent one-fourth that for a perfectly functional Toyota Camry.

It's why people get tattoos of Harley-Davidson, Nike, and P90X. Why in the world would anyone ink a logo permanently on their skin? What would drive them to even consider such a thing? It ain't logic!

If you want to maximize your leads growth, make sure that you're evoking an emotional response from your audience.

Improving Business Performance through Creativity

So, let's evoke an emotional response from your target audience. But where to start?

Glad you asked. The best place to start is by injecting creativity into the DNA of your marketing.

As mentioned, I built my first website several years before Google even existed. As the digital marketing field evolved and matured through the years, marketers seemed to become all-consumed with optimization and hacks. Increasing immediate conversions became an industry-wide obsession.

One thing I've long written about is that prior to optimization, you need excellent ideas. After all, optimizing what's mediocre will never maximize your results. Instead, it will get you optimized mediocrity, which is not too thrilling, right?

It's much easier and scalable to execute exceptional marketing and to then start optimizing.

If you think about it, creativity underscores all business progress. It simply cannot be commoditized. It's what sparks the greatest growth. It's the most sustainable competitive advantage.

When you look at highly successful businesses, you typically find a lot of creativity at the core. Scott Dorsey, Co-founder and CEO of the email marketing software company ExactTarget, for example, credited the company's success to *creativity*, pointing to its impact on everything from product development to customer acquisition. He went so far as to say that creativity was "the key ingredient". All of this creativity led to the company's $2.5 billion acquisition by Salesforce.[5]

Dorsey isn't the only one who feels this way.

McKinsey surveyed more than 200 CMOs and senior marketing executives. They also tracked the business performance of the associated companies.

What they found will surprise those who have been heads down in data for the past 15 years while ignoring other aspects of marketing.

According to McKinsey's study, marketers who have united data and creativity ("integrators") grow revenue at twice the rate of companies that manage data and creativity separately.[6]

In other words, creativity is equally important to business growth as data, and if your marketing team ignores creativity, your results will suffer. Badly.

This insight aligns with previous McKinsey findings on the impact of creativity on a brand's bottom line. McKinsey found that the most creative companies outperform peers financially.

The management consulting firm found, in fact, that the most creative companies exhibited four business practices that translated into higher business value:

- They inject creativity and innovation into daily activities
- They become customer fanatics
- They translate insight into action fast
- They adapt based on what's working and what's not[7]

And it's not only McKinsey that found that creativity fuels better business performance. Forrester Consulting came to the same conclusion. In a Forrester study commissioned by Adobe, it was found that companies that foster creativity achieve significantly more revenue growth than peers. Specifically, companies from the study that foster creativity achieved at least 10 percent revenue growth at 3.5X the rate of companies that do not prioritize creativity.[8]

In another study that polled more than 3,600 companies with at least $100 million in annual revenue, Tenovos found that enterprises that emphasize creativity significantly outperform their less creative counterparts. In the study, 100 percent of respondents confirmed that creativity considerably improves top-line growth while also strengthening customer loyalty and increasing overall profitability.[9]

Based on the McKinsey, Forrester, and Tenovos research, it's clear that creativity improves business performance. The next question is, how can your marketing organization spur greater creativity and innovation. Let's dig in...

Dismantling the Eureka Myth

So, you can see the value in lateral thinking and being creative in your lead generation efforts. But *how* do you generate creative ideas?

Our society tends to prop up the notion that the best, new, innovative ideas come from isolated moments of inspiration. But do they?

The lightbulb signifies a great idea. We shout "Eureka" when a powerful new thought clarifies our vision. We celebrate epiphanies. We treat an "aha" moment as a one-time breakthrough. We celebrate this concept throughout our culture.

However, as Steven Johnson shows us in his book, *Where Good Ideas Come From: The Natural History of Innovation*, the best ideas are typically iterative, take shape over periods of time, and occur in the "adjacent possible" (relying directly on previous knowledge). Innovative ideas often have long incubation periods, as Johnson calls them.

Instead of ideas popping like popcorn, they form more like a stew. Ingredients are mixed together, and the more you heat the stew and stir the pot, they form the possibility of what's new.

Without first having the ingredients, it would have been impossible to cook that particular stew.

Johnson explains that the real secret to innovation is to connect ideas. It's in the cross-pollination of ideas that the new and previously unimagined emerge.

In the book he gives the example of GPS, the Global Positioning System, which was originally developed for military use. It is now the platform upon which countless innovations have been hatched and on which many location-based services have been launched.

But GPS didn't come about overnight. Far from it…

Stumbling Upon GPS (It Was A Total Accident)

In the book, Johnson tells the story of the evolution of GPS, which was accidentally developed by scientists at the Applied Physics Lab associated with John Hopkins University messing around with a microwave receiver.

When the Russians launched Sputnik on October 4, 1957, the scientists started chatting and asking if anyone had tried listening to the trajectory of the satellite through space. After a couple of hours of playing around with a microwave receiver, they started to pick up the signal at 20 MHz. They realized that what they were doing might be historic, and so they started to record the signal.

They noticed that the frequency of radio signals transmitted by the satellite increased as it approached the Earth and correspondingly decreased when it moved away, an occurrence known as the Doppler Effect. Through this understanding they were able to track the speed of the satellite, and therefore, its location. After three weeks or so, they were able to track Sputnik's exact trajectory around the planet.

A couple of weeks later their boss asked them if it might be possible to do the opposite — using the position of satellites to track the exact position of something on Earth. They thought about it and then realized that it would actually be *easier* to track objects in that way. Their boss was relieved, as he was building nuclear submarines but wasn't able to figure out how to ensure the accuracy of missile launches, as he couldn't accurately track the location of the subs in the ocean.

This is how GPS was born.

Six satellites orbiting the planet in the 1960s were able to pinpoint the submarines' location within minutes. In the 1970s, the Department of Defense launched its first Navigation System with Timing and Ranging (NAVSTAR) satellite.

Later, President Reagan opened the GPS platform, unleashing a wave of innovation and new businesses built on top of the platform. In other words, without the platform itself, these businesses never would have been created. Think of the navigation system in your car. Or the many location-based services on your smartphone. Or, all of the geo-based marketing opportunities at your fingertips as a marketer. Today, applications based on GPS technology include those in mining, aviation, surveying, agriculture, marine, and more.

It didn't happen with a sudden "Eureka!" moment. Rather, all of these GPS-powered technologies were invented through an iterative process of different ideas leading to new ideas, and those leading to still newer ideas.

So, when brainstorming internally and committing to creativity in daily activities at your company, remember that innovation is not merely jumping in a conference room and having one brainstorming session. Rather, it's the cultural ecosystem that you create that fosters newer and newer ideas, that ultimately lead again to newer and newer ideas.

Creativity is an iterative process. It's a culture. It's a way of life.

Cross-pollinating For Stronger Innovation

When all you have is a hammer, everything looks like a nail.

It's unclear who originally said this, but it's oh, so, accurate.

The Einstellung Effect is a cognitive bias in which a person (say, a marketer) is predisposed to solve a problem in the specific way they're used to doing it. Whatever they've done in the past is going to be their inclination for solving new challenges. This cognitive bias prevents marketers from seeing better or simpler solutions to problems.

This is why you see organizations doing the same marketing over and over. Sure, they probably tweak it here or there, but essentially it's the same as what they've done before.

A solution to break the mold and achieve better results?

Cross-pollination.

A key element to marketing breakthroughs is bringing the "outside" in. Cross-pollination is a powerful force, and one I firmly believe makes all the difference in lateral thinking that transcends the ordinary and helps you trailblaze new paths towards stronger results. It's why industries or geographic areas with a higher population of immigrants tend to generate more patents.

In the paper *Immigration and the Rise of American Ingenuity*, University of Chicago's Ufuk Akcigit and John Grigsby and

Harvard Business School's Tom Nicholas examined industries during the timeframe between 1940 and 2000 with higher percentages of foreign-born inventors. What they found was that these industries produced more patents and inventions than others.[10]

The same phenomenon was evidenced when the U.S. experienced an influx of Jewish immigrants from Nazi Germany. The article *German Jewish Emigres and US Invention* by Petra Moser, Alessandra Voena, and Fabian Waldinger in *The American Economic Review* shows that the Jewish immigrants revolutionized science in the U.S. After they arrived, fields with a large number of these individuals experienced a 31 percent increase in patents.[11]

When Meagen Eisenberg was CMO at the database platform company MongoDB, she shared with me that in order to achieve marketing innovation, B2B marketers should pay attention to consumer marketing. What are consumers responding strongly to today, and how can you apply it to what you're doing in attracting B2B audiences? What's going on in direct mail? How about at the grocery store? Why are people clicking on what they're clicking on in social media?

In this way, cross-pollination is a powerful force for innovation.

Make sure your lead generation ideation process includes cross-pollination. Without it, you're bound to stick to what you've been doing (perhaps with slight adjustments), or what the competition is doing, or "best practices". When you do that, you underperform.

Don't underperform.

A Lateral Thinking Framework For Your Lead Generation

As you can see, if you are to inject lateral thinking and creativity into the very DNA of your lead generation initiatives, you're able to achieve better results. However, the most powerful new ideas tend to come out of an iterative process, not a one-time, big-bang, eureka-type moment.

To ensure you're thinking through your lead generation options and coming up with creative, potentially game-changing ideas, use the following framework:

1. Identify the specific problem you're trying to solve, or the specific goal you aim to achieve. Although with brainstorming you want as open a mind as possible, in terms of the problem or goal it's actually beneficial to be as specific as possible.
2. Develop a brainstorming brief. It doesn't need to be anything formal or stuffy. It can even be written in a Slack message or email. But it's important to clarify the basics for everyone involved. In the brief, specify the ultimate goals and outcomes. Define the audience. Explain the need for change. What are the repercussions if you don't change? Lay out any ground rules of the brainstorming itself. What are the parameters or structures you'll work within? What are the KPIs by which you'll measure the success of any changes?
3. OK, now it's time to brainstorm ideas with no constraints. Be open to ALL ideas.
4. Keep going until you have at least 35 new ideas. I know it's a lot, but trust me on this. You're likely to come up with a handful of ideas that may be good, but not great,

with the first suggestions. It's only when you pound on the problem, digging deeper and exploring more broadly, that you're more likely going to stumble upon something groundbreaking. Go for as many ideas as you can, and you're sure to come up with some true winners.
5. As you brainstorm, build a matrix outlining the following factors for each idea: Cost, Timeframe, Ease (Lift), Revenue Potential, and ROI. (Our team at Stratabeat uses a Green-Yellow-Red coding system for the first four factors, and then an actual projected dollar amount for ROI.)
6. Take a break. Come back another day and brainstorm again after everyone has had a chance to digest the topic and all the ideas from the earlier session. See how far you can take it.
7. Make sure every idea is documented in your matrix detailing Cost, Timeframe, Ease, Revenue Potential, and ROI.
8. Based on the matrix, narrow down your list of ideas to the top three that will deliver the greatest ROI. (Note, if your priority is to stick within a certain budget or timeframe, etc., then allow those to guide your decision making.) It's important that your final list is no more than three ideas, so that you can focus on exceptional execution and not dilute your efforts.

To take your ideation to a completely new level, inject ideas from the "outside" into your brainstorming. Here's how to do that:

1. List all the "best practices" in your industry for the problem you're trying to solve. What are your

competitors doing, for example? What has your own business been doing? Now, cross out these best practices and consider doing the opposite.
2. Bring in folks from other divisions or departments in your company. What creative ideas might they have?
3. Study other industries. Read case studies and success stories from other industries. Bring in a consultant. How can you cross-pollinate what they are doing into your solution?
4. Invite someone from outside of your industry to brainstorm ideas with you.
5. Brainstorm with some of your clients. Tap into their brainpower, and learn from them.

Chapter Summary

At a time when data, optimization, and marketing "hacks" are often the centerpiece of a marketing program, remember that to achieve remarkable results, the best ideas win. Creativity, innovation, and lateral thinking are your secret weapons for maximum marketing returns.

Yes, data and optimization are also essential. This cannot be stressed enough.

But creativity is going to be the spark that ignites transformative results and enables you to cut through all the noise. Focus on creativity, lateral thinking, and innovation in your business, and in turn, watch your leads and revenue grow.

- If you're looking for a 5 percent incremental gain in marketing results, you have lots of options. But if you're looking for exponential gains, turn to lateral thinking and creativity.

- What worked for you in the past is probably not what's going to lead to new exponential growth now. Do something different.
- As Reid Hoffman points out, the best ideas are often the most laughable.
- For breakthrough results, try doing the exact opposite of what you've done in the past.
- Understand that everyone is irrational. So is your target audience.
- Don't rely on logic and reasoning. Evoke an emotional response from your prospective customers for maximum impact.
- McKinsey, Forrester, and Tenovo found that the most creative companies achieve greater financial performance than their peers. Creativity is a competitive advantage that helps you achieve breakthrough business results
- The eureka moment is a myth. According to author Steven Johnson, the best ideas are typically iterative, take shape over periods of time, and occur in the realm of the "adjacent possible".
- The real secret of innovation is to connect ideas. It's in the cross-pollination of ideas that the new and previously unimagined emerge.
- Use the lateral thinking framework outlined in this chapter to help you identify three powerful new lead generation ideas that you'll launch and test.

2

TRANSFORMING YOUR WEBSITE INTO AN UNSTOPPABLE LEADS ENGINE

Using IP detection, our team at Stratabeat noticed a site visitor returning to our website over and over. They visited the website a half dozen times. However, there were no conversions during their visits. With the IP data in hand, we noticed that they were very interested in content marketing and SEO. We found the right contacts at the company in LinkedIn, and so we reached out and started engaging with them accordingly.

Over the course of the next two months, they visited our website 24 times. During this time, we reached out by email and provided them with a number of links and each time tracked exactly what they clicked on, what they didn't click, where they spent the most time on our website and even within each page. This dictated each new conversation we had with them. By understanding their interests as proven through the data, we customized every interaction.

We even had videos of their visits to our site thanks to our implementation of behavioral analytics software. The videos recorded their screen movements as they navigated throughout the site, but this gave us a clear picture of their experience during each visit.

Capitalizing on all of this information, we customized our messaging, communications, and engagement with the company. The end result? We closed the deal and landed a new client.

In this way, we use our website as a strategic advantage for our business. We look at it as an insight platform that enables us to target the right people at the right time with the right message. Even if they don't fill out a form or otherwise provide their email address while on the site, we still actively conduct lead generation.

Is your website a strategic advantage for your brand? Is it a high-performance lead generation engine? Is it a game changer?

Or is it just "meh"?

What Does It Mean To Rethink Your Website?

If you want your website to be a lead generation engine, then rethink your site. It should be a dynamic command center of audience insight and interaction. You should be actively reviewing the data from your site and then acting on it. This might mean conducting new tests, or it might mean updating content, or it might mean changing your CTAs.

Too many companies set up web pages and then forget about them. Too many marketing teams publish content but then never return to optimize it. It's a classic case of "set it and forget it". I see it all the time.

You may be doing certain things to generate leads, but it's highly likely that you are missing others. There are always more opportunities to improve what you're doing, and opportunities for new strategies and tactics to bring in additional leads.

As an agency, we see a great number of B2B websites. On top of this, we maintain a database of hundreds of B2B websites, where we evaluate a number of aspects of each site and identify trends and correlations.

The truth is that most B2B websites are lacking in multiple areas where lead generation should be strong.

Want a website that generates more leads? Read on, and learn how to transform your website from a collection of stale web pages into a strategic platform that's optimized from multiple angles for more effective lead gen.

What's In It For Me?

If you want your website to maximize conversions and leads, it should be framed from the perspective of the site visitor ("What's in it for me?").

B2B site visitors are self interested. They come to your site looking to achieve an objective or solve a problem or eliminate pain. Simple as that.

They are not there to learn about how many employees you have. Nor do they care where your offices are located (unless they are looking for a specific address to find and meet with you). Nor do they care that you have a bring-your-dogs-to-the-office policy.

What they care about is acquiring more customers, or driving efficiency gains, or beating competitors. They care about their own stuff, not yours.

So, in your website, stop talking about yourselves. Seriously!

Instead, talk about them. Talk about all they will achieve by hiring you, using your services, or purchasing your products.

Here's a simple check you can do in the next ten minutes. Go to your website and see how often you are using "Me" language. Meaning, how often are you focusing on your company, your products, your services, your technology, your methodology, your culture, etc.?

Now, instead, what if you were to replace these instances with "You" (the site visitor) language? What if you flipped the script and wrote like this instead: "Are you looking for a better, easier way to manage your contacts without all the hair pulling?" or "See how quickly you can cut your time in half getting email campaigns out the door," etc.

If you're finding it difficult to do so and you find your team defaulting to talk of your products/services and internally-oriented topics, then perhaps your brand is not delivering enough value to your customers.

The Customer Journey

An effective way to drive more leads through your website is to understand the customer journey more deeply for each audience segment.

First, define your audience segments. Then, define buyer personas for each segment. This is important so that you customize your marketing for each segment or persona, making your marketing resonate more powerfully.

A typical B2B persona might include:

- Job title and role
- Who they report to
- Department
- Size of company
- Industry
- Goals
- Problems, obstacles, and frustrations
- Worries
- Factors for promotion
- Budget
- Priorities
- News sources

From there, walk through the customer journey for each persona. For example, ask yourself:

- What caused them to start looking for information, an answer, or a solution?
- What emotions are they feeling when they start the journey?
- Where do they go online prior to visiting your site when this issue arises, and why?
- What are each of the steps in the journey? What pushes them from one step to another?
- What are the specific questions they are asking themselves at each step?
- What are the specific questions they are asking themselves when they arrive on your website?
- What actions should they take on your site in order to have a better user experience?
- After they leave your site, where do they go, and why?

Without understanding the customer journey for each persona, you're guessing. It's really as simple as that. You're guessing what should be in your website. You're guessing at the messaging. You're guessing at your offerings. You're guessing at the positioning of your offerings. You're guessing what would really solve their problems. You're guessing how to convert them to a lead. And you're guessing at how to deliver the best possible experience.

I'd second guess that strategy…

Knowing Their Questions

When they arrive at your website, do you know what they're thinking? Do you know the questions racing through their minds?

Ensuring your website answers what's on the minds of your site visitors is more critical than you may understand. It all boils down to the relationship between their questions and how they will consume the information in your site.

Alfred Lukyanovich Yarbus, a Russian psychologist and author of the book *Eye Movements and Vision*, conducted eye tracking studies that revealed that individuals consume information differently depending on what's going through their minds at the time.

In one study, he showed individuals a painting and asked each individual a question prior to revealing the painting. Depending on the question asked, their eyes would look at different parts of the painting.

For example:

- If the question was "How old are the people in the painting?", the viewer would look at the faces of the individuals in the painting.
- If, however, Yarbus asked, "What is their status in society?", they would look at their clothing (and would not look at their faces).
- In the case he asked, "What were the activities of the family prior to the visitor's arrival?", they would look at the table, piano, the person playing the piano and the person opening the door. (Only a tiny fraction of the time was spent looking at their faces or their clothing.)

What Yarbus' studies reveal is that your site visitors will tend to filter out anything deemed extraneous to their mission. Instead, they will focus on what their brain decides will help it discern the narrative logic to the question they are trying to answer.

This is what's happening when your site visitors arrive on your website, blog, or landing page.

What are the specific questions each persona is asking precisely when they hit your site?

Document these questions, and then make sure that you're answering them very clearly. If you don't make it clear that your page (or website overall) delivers these answers, you may see a high abandonment rate among your site visitors.

If you don't know the questions in their minds as they hit your site, do voice of the customer (VoC) research, as explained below.

Capturing VoC

Your website is an effective vehicle to inform your site visitors. However, it works the other way, too.

Are you using your website to learn more about your prospective customers? Many businesses completely overlook this and miss out on a great deal of valuable information.

Rethink your website. Use it as a microscope into the minds of your audience. Use it as an audience insight engine.

For example, onsite surveys are one of my favorite tools to capture VoC, which, simply put, is an expression of how your audience is feeling about their expectations and experiences related to your products, services, or brand. VoC can be used for greater understanding of and empathy towards your customers.

In the Stratabeat blog, when we run surveys, we typically will have at least 10 surveys running concurrently. We find that including contextually relevant surveys with what's on the respective page increases engagement and response rates.

For example, if it's a blog post about SEO, then the survey is about SEO. If the post is about behavioral intelligence instead, the survey is about behavioral intelligence. In this way, we're asking the right questions to an audience that has pre-qualified themselves as being relevant.

After all, it would be less effective and would probably lead to low quality data if we have a survey about SEO in a post about emotional marketing, IP detection, or heat mapping.

Our blog surveys are inline, meaning they appear in the column of text that the reader is already consuming. We find this to be a natural experience and less intrusive than a pop-up survey.

That's not to say that it's not worth testing pop-up surveys. Those can also be useful.

If you use pop-up surveys, though, I'd recommend that you employ the same level of contextual relevance as Stratabeat uses with our blog surveys. Make sure that what's popping up on the screen is highly relevant to the particular page.

Otherwise you're simply going to annoy the heck out of your site visitors.

ANOTHER EFFECTIVE WAY TO gather VoC is through industry surveys. This would be a survey that you can offer anywhere where your audience is online. For example, you could email the survey to your entire database, or have strategic partners share it with their mailing lists, or have industry publications offer it, etc.

For one of our clients in the healthcare industry, we conducted a survey that generated roughly 3,500 responses. This provided us with invaluable insight into the challenges, frustrations, and needs of the target audience, registered nurses. On top of this, the marketing that came out of the survey resulted in our client being featured on national TV five times within a year. (Don't underestimate what a single survey can do for your business!)

What's critically important when conducting a survey is to deviate from what most do, which is stick to only quantitative data and analysis. Sure, this is easier and more efficient to collect and analyze.

However, the gold is in the qualitative information they provide you. Our formula is to use easily quantifiable data for all of your survey questions except the final one or two. Then you give the survey recipient the opportunity to unleash everything they've been bottling up about the topic.

Let them have at it. Don't limit them.

The feedback and stories you will get in return are priceless, and will no doubt provide you with information that your competitors don't have.

∽

WANT ANOTHER SECRET?

Conduct an *annual* survey. This can be a state of the industry survey, or any topic that would be of interest to your target audience on a recurring basis.

For example, Food Engineering has conducted an annual State of Food Manufacturing survey and report every year since 2014. For one of Stratabeat's clients, we launched an annual survey in the software internationalization industry, driving leads through not only the survey itself, but the accompanying report, webinar, blog posts, and social promotions. It's something that can be done in almost any industry.

By running the same survey every year, you OWN that information in your industry. Everyone expects it to come from you and they turn to you each year. If anyone even tried to copy you, it would be obvious that they were doing a copycat study. By publishing an annual survey, you are able to more easily gain media attention and exposure, as well.

∽

SURVEYS ARE great for generating leads, as well. Really great.

The fintech company Provenir, which offers a risk analytics and decisioning platform that makes risk analytics faster and simpler for financial institutions, uses surveys for lead generation as effectively as any company I've come across. Then VP of Marketing, Sales Ops, and Inside Sales, Adi Reske, explained to me that they were able to secure 300 responses through the company's main onsite survey within a year. About one third of these resulted in new leads for the business.

If you think about that, it's brilliant. Reske and her team placed the survey on the site, which cost them nothing, and then sat back and let the leads come to them. The value of 100 pre-qualified leads? Priceless. Not only did they raise their hands to be contacted by sales, they also had already provided insight into their needs based on their survey responses.

And for the other respondents who did not raise their hand, Reske found their feedback quite valuable as well, as it offered an additional 10-15 data points in each survey for understanding their audience deeper.

What other website vehicle is simple to deploy, costs you practically nothing, and generates audience insights and leads on an ongoing basis? Surveys are a powerful marketing tool, yet too many companies are not using them or are constructing them incorrectly or are placing them on pages that have nothing to do with the content on that page.

SIMILAR TO SURVEYS, conversational marketing through live chat and AI-based chatbots is another way to capture VoC while driving leads growth. The rapidly growing software company

Drift is a case in point. As mentioned earlier, Drift is a revenue acceleration platform. However, at its core, it's a conversational marketing software company. Drift used chatbots on its own website to engage with site visitors when it removed all lead forms for its downloadable content. In other words, if someone came upon an ebook on the site, they could just click and access it rather than needing to submit a form with their contact information.

Drift was the first SaaS that I'm aware of to ungate all of its content resources, and it was highly controversial at the time. But in my discussions with former Chief Brand Officer (and VP of Marketing prior to that), Dave Gerhardt, the move unleashed Drift's growth.

Drift has been creative with their use of chatbots. For example, they've used a "three visit" rule to turn blog visitors into qualified leads for sales. The way it worked is that a chatbot in the blog appeared only to readers who had dropped by at least three times. They figured that if site visitors that engaged in the blog, there's a good chance they'd be interested in learning more about Drift. They therefore invited these individuals to see a product demo. If they were interested, the bot displayed the salesperson's calendar and they could then book the demo right then and there.

Bots can be fantastic at driving leads, as they eliminate all of the traditional back and forth you find with forms and email communications. For example, a high percentage of site visitors on Drift's pricing page who open the initial message have started an actual conversation with one of Drift's sales reps.

Jeanne Hopkins was CMO at Ipswitch, Inc., an IT management software company, when she informed me of the success she, as well, had been having with chatbots. Success is putting it lightly.

Ipswitch actually added an incremental $1 million to its sales pipeline with interactive chat as the company's number one source of leads within the first three months of installing Drift on merely one page of their site. Wow!

To be as successful as possible with chat, be sure to:

- Figure out how you'll staff your conversations. Larger companies often have live teams responsible, while smaller companies might implement a combination of live teams along with automated chatbots. Some use live teams during business hours, and bots during off hours. See what works for you.
- Whoever is responsible for communicating through chat, make sure they are welcoming, responsive, and engaging.
- Create playbooks for different pages in your site. Make sure that the chats that are triggered are contextually relevant to what's on that particular page.
- Optimize those playbooks over time.
- Refine your process for routing prospects to your salespeople.

ANOTHER VOC TECHNIQUE TO unearth the questions that your audience is asking is to use question identification tools. Tools are continually evolving, and new ones are being introduced all the time. At the time of this writing, though, BuzzSumo is a useful tool that captures the questions being asked in Quora or millions of Q&A and forum sites online. Alternatively, you could use tools such as AnswerSocrates.com or Answer The Public to see questions that are being asked online. Or you could lean on

Google itself by reviewing the People Also Ask box (Google's built-in questions engine) when available in the search results.

The point is, VoC is essential if you want a website that answers audience members' questions and helps them achieve their objectives. And as we saw with Yarbus' eye-tracking studies, having a website that immediately addresses the questions running through their minds will help you to connect with them more directly and deliver an experience that matches their intent.

Your Hook

As you collect VoC data and uncover questions they are asking as they hit your website, learn the deepest pain points of your audience and uncover their most critical goals for success. Then take this information, craft your hook, and feature it in your website.

- What makes your solutions different?
- Why is it so important that they use your solutions?
- What's your differentiation as a brand?
- Beyond your known competitors, what about all the online options?
- Beyond your known competitors, how do your solutions compare to the status quo (your often forgotten silent competitor)?

Without clear differentiation, your job of converting site visitors into leads is going to be a whole heck of a lot harder.

As an agency, we're often surprised by the number of companies that come to us without clear differentiation. If your differentiation is not clear in your website, you are going to have serious problems. And your lead gen is going to suffer. I write that unequivocally.

Companies we meet for the first time sometimes say, "Our people are our differentiation." We hear that one a lot. Well, that's typically a load of crap. Sorry, it's not your people. Unless you can tell me everything about the people at all of your competitors, and unless you can tell me about their ideas, work ethic, and recent accomplishments, you're making this one up. You're hoping your people are better, but you have no proof.

Some say their technology is their differentiation. Fine, but what happens when your competitors leapfrog your technology? Then, are you saying no one should purchase from you anymore? Probably not, right? Based on history, any company that has had a technology advantage, eventually doesn't. So claiming that technology by itself is your differentiation is a risky proposition.

Plus, to your buyer, your technology is actually irrelevant in most cases. Sure, it perhaps needs to be compatible with other internal systems, but the reason they purchase from you is the same reason people buy, say, cordless drills. It's not because the manufacturing technology in your drill was superior. It's because your drill helps them drill more holes, drive screws, and mix paint (when outfitted with specialty mixing bits) faster and more easily. (Your technology simply enabled them to achieve this.)

So what is your hook?

I'll tell you from experience that the strongest hooks are customer-focused. They are substantive. They are also simple and immediately understandable.

In behavioral economics, there are various cognitive biases. One of these biases is the "Focusing Effect". In developing your hook, you need to not only be aware of this, but to address it head on.

People (your buyers) tend to focus and latch on to a single aspect of your product or service, instead of understanding it holistically with all of its many features, benefits, and nuances. If you want your hook to be more effective, don't spray your audience with every possible detail about your offerings.

It's counterintuitive, but you should actually describe your product or service less.

Simplify your message. Focus on the most important outcome for your audience. Your hook will be more powerful.

Whatever your hook, be sure it's customer-focused, simple, and substantive.

The Power of Great Design

When you think of your website, your mind may initially think of your message or perhaps the marketing of your products or services.

The reality is that your site design is a critical, foundational element in the success of your website.

Stratabeat maintains a database of hundreds of B2B websites. We record a range of information about each site, from overall traffic to organic traffic, quality of site design, the state of SEO, deployment of CTAs, the presence of case studies, and more. In our analysis of the websites in our database, we found that B2B websites with high quality design attract exponentially more traffic than sites with poor design.

Is this correlation or causation?

I think it's both.

The websites with high traffic, raving reviews, online shares, positive word of mouth, and passionate advocates tend to have a professional design. When individuals promote a piece of content, they are associating themselves with that content to some degree. It therefore follows that they logically gravitate towards those content pieces that have a higher design aesthetic and make them look better.

It's a case of a rising tide lifting all boats. A great-looking website boosts the performance of any campaign you may run. Want more people excited about your brand and telling others about it? Want more returning and recurring traffic? Spend time and energy ensuring a high-quality visual aesthetic for your website, and it will pay off in more ways than one.

What makes for good web design? There are a wide range of factors, but here are some of the most fundamental:

- Aesthetically pleasing to your site visitors
- Adheres to a defined brand color palette
- Easy to understand and navigate (high cognitive fluency)
- Highly visual
- Visually consistent
- Clean design
- Plenty of whitespace
- Legible fonts
- Avoids equally-weighted presentation of elements
- Uses deviation to draw attention to important elements
- Avoids large blocks of text (outside of blog and similar types of content)

- Supports your business effectively
- Guides site visitors to the achievement of their site objectives
- Etc.

Cognitive Fluency

From a neuroscience perspective, our brains are hard-wired to enjoy information processing when it's easy and intuitive. And so if you're looking to improve the lead generation results from your website, focus on improving your site visitors' ability to immediately and intuitively understand what's presented and what they should do next.

In a study by Google, the company uncovered that site visitors are judging a website's design within merely 50 milliseconds, and to a degree even within 17 milliseconds. In other words, when your site visitors arrive at your site, they judge it in the blink of an eye.[12]

"Cognitive fluency" is the measure by which one's brain processes information. A high level of cognitive fluency means that something is easy for your site visitors' brains to process, whereas a low level means that something is relatively difficult to understand, decipher, or to get through.

Cognitive fluency impacts not only your brain, but how you feel about something. In other words, the sensation of ease or difficulty in our thinking guides us to feel a certain way about it. If your site visitor has difficulty figuring out how to find what they are seeking on your site, guess what? A low level of cognitive fluency. Worse, it can result in a poor brand experience and negative feelings towards your brand as a whole.

You can see the effects of cognitive fluency throughout society. Psychologists have found that shares in companies with easier-to-pronounce names perform better than those with difficult-to-pronounce names. Even just changing the font on a page to something more legible can alter people's judgments about the veracity of the statement.

If you want to facilitate lead generation in your website, make your site easy to understand and easy to navigate.

Conversion Funnels

In order to turn website visitors into leads, you need to convert them. One of the most efficient ways to do that is through the construction of conversion funnels and conversion events.

When someone lands on your website, what should they do next? Do you know? Can you be specific? More importantly, is it clear to them?

One enterprise software client we worked with constructed the top of their home page with a CTA to request a demo. Although this may be an excellent CTA at the end of a conversion funnel, it's far too early to ask them to do this when they've only just arrived on your site and don't even know anything about your product yet.

Sure enough, when we examined the behavioral analytics of their home page, no one was clicking on the "request a demo" CTA at the top of the page.

The problem? There was no funnel. Site visitors didn't have sufficient information yet to decide if a demo was worth their time.

So, how do you build funnels within your website?

Well, first, let's define the three different funnels you should build:

- Customer journey
- Website journey
- Offer journey

We spoke about the customer journey earlier in this chapter.

The website journey is the funnel they traverse from first landing on your site until conversion event. The offer journey is a subset of the website journey, focused on the time you make your compelling offer.

Think of any purchase as a funnel. When someone arrives on your site, something triggered them to feel a need. What was that trigger?

Here's where audience segmentation and personas come into play in a major way. Think of your different audience members, and ask yourself if each one would know where to go and what to do on your website.

Now that you're ready to address your audience according to their respective segments, personas, and problems, it's time to deploy your respective hooks. Ultimately, what are the hardest-hitting reasons why they should purchase from you? Why are you better than competitors? Why are you better than the status quo?

Develop a schematic of the step-by-step process that each audience segment takes as they progress from arriving on your site all the way to the ultimate conversion event.

From different landing pages within your site, have you thought through where they should go as a next step in the journey? Is it clear to them? Is it easy? Is it compelling? Are you building brand love along the way?

Continue like this through each step in the process.

Landing Pages

Landing pages are often the final step in a conversion funnel. This is where you'll often find the offer journey.

To increase leads from specific campaigns, it's useful to develop and deploy individual landing pages fully customized for the campaign. The look-and-feel, the messaging, and any offers on the campaign should be mirrored in the landing page. The more they are in alignment, the more intuitive the experience for the person clicking through.

Landing pages are effective at converting visitors into leads because of their topical focus. Plus, you can remove navigation on the page to limit their options and guide them to a single conversion event on the page.

To make your landing pages more effective, follow these recommendations:

- Keep the design clean and minimalistic.
- Use a concise, compelling headline at the top of the page.
- Pair the headline with a series of persuasive subheadings.
- Speak clearly to the pain and frustration that landing page visitors are feeling.

- Reinforce the pain they will feel in the case of inaction, as well.
- Focus on benefits instead of features.
- Include social proof, such as client logos or publications in which your brand has been featured. You can also include client testimonials.
- Keep your forms short, with as few fields as necessary while at the same time satisfying your needs to qualify leads.
- Clarify what happens after they submit the form.
- A/B test different aspects of your landing page. Go with the winners and drop losers. Rinse and repeat.

Calls-to-Action (CTAs)

CTAs are a strategic tool to take your site visitor from a passive to an active state. Use CTAs throughout your website to drive them to actions that will provide them with contextually relevant added value.

Treat CTAs as part of your salesforce. With CTAs, you'll generate more engagement, sign-ups, and leads.

Include CTAs throughout your website and blog. Wherever you have content, you can have CTAs. It always baffles me when I come across a B2B site that lacks CTAs or has very few of them. It's like having a store but no salespeople inside to help guide people with the final step in their journey.

And don't limit yourself. You can include more than one CTA in a single page. Depending on the length and nature of your page or post, you can sometimes include four, five, or more. (Really!)

The value of someone who signs up for your mailing list is far greater than someone who is on your site who doesn't. Similarly, someone who downloads your playbook is more valuable than someone who doesn't. A site visitor who contacts you to learn more about your services is worth more than someone who simply abandons the site.

CTAs are one of the most important aspects of a B2B website, yet too many companies treat them as an afterthought, consequently limiting their site results.

Take the time to think through your CTAs and to test them. For example, even something as simple as testing the phrasing of the CTA copy can be eye-opening. Should it be "Download Your Playbook" or "Download My Playbook" or "Download Playbook"? The only way to know is through testing.

Same with CTA button colors. Try different contrasting colors to see what generates the most conversions. As you're testing colors, make sure that your designer is aware that an estimated 300 million people worldwide are impacted by red-green color vision deficiency, or "color blindness".

Another useful test would be the size of the CTAs. For one client offering a database of business contracts for sale, we needed to make searching the site the main CTA and to place a massive search bar and CTA right on the home page in order to guide visitors to the most important action on the site.

Sometimes, although it's counterintuitive, taking them through a multi-step process instead works best. For one client in the financial services space, we found that conversion rates increased when we created a multi-step interactive wizard instead of a regular site form. Sometimes simply getting them engaged and committed builds the momentum you need for them to follow through with the final conversion.

As one of our tests in the Stratabeat website, we started displaying a pop-up CTA asking our first-time blog readers to opt in to our mailing list — but only if they had scrolled down 70 percent of the post first.

We thought that if they were finding enough value to keep scrolling and scrolling down the page, then they would probably find value in our email blasts.

In this way, *behaviorally-based CTAs* can be very effective in that they align with the digital body language of your blog readers. The timing is everything. You hit them with a CTA at precisely the time that their behavior indicates they would be most receptive to the offer. When Stratabeat instituted the behaviorally-based CTA in our blog, mailing list opt-ins increased by more than 300 percent. Booyah!

How else can you implement behaviorally-based CTAs? Well, try displaying the CTAs based on the following factors:

- The page they visit
- A page navigation sequence
- How long they are on the page
- The time they've been on the website
- Inactivity time
- Interactions with your initial CTA (e.g., show a second CTA at a later time)
- Their cookies (the web/browser kind, not chocolate chip cookies or snickerdoodles)
- When they are about to leave the website
- If they return to the site after visiting certain pages without a conversion

Beyond behaviorally-based CTAs, you can also include static CTA banners or even inline text CTAs. Stratabeat has been doing this for years in our blog, whether asking them to contact us, or whether promoting our *Rethink Your Marketing* book, one of our playbooks, or an upcoming event. It simply makes sense to capitalize on the real estate on the page to drive additional results for the business.

One key to greater success is to always make your CTAs contextually relevant to the page. The other key is to A/B test your CTAs as much as possible.

Evoking an Emotional Response

As mentioned earlier, if you want to start generating more engagement and conversions from your website, look to evoke an emotional response.

If you recall from the prior chapter, the neuroscientist Antonio Damasio found that emotions are a core ingredient in decision making (including purchase decisions). People first decide with their emotions. Only then do they apply logic to rationalize the decisions.

So, if you want your blog readers to decide to download your lead magnet, register for your upcoming webinar, subscribe to your mailing list, or contact you to talk with sales, etc., evoke an emotional response from them. Otherwise, you're making it mentally difficult for them to take action.

Don't make the same mistake that many B2B websites do and publish accurate but boring content. Make it interesting, make it surprising, make it differentiated, make it exciting, and make it compelling. Do what it takes to generate an emotional response.

Building Trust

Do you like canned laughter? No, of course not. No one does. Even the TV executives who require its inclusion in your shows can't stand it.

Then why in the world do they continue to insist on its use in just about every sitcom?

In a word, social proof.

What researchers have found is that when people hear canned laughter during a TV show, they laugh LOUDER and they laugh LONGER. They actually enjoy the show more. It's outrageous to think about, but it's true.

Let me explain.

In his book *Influence: The Psychology of Persuasion*, Robert Cialdini highlights six core methods of influencing someone's behavior. Among these, "Consensus" is especially key for building trust with your audience.

Put another way, social proof. If you want to influence someone or persuade them in a certain direction, showing them that lots of people are already doing it is a powerful driver of human behavior. I took the canned laughter example from Cialdini's book.

How does this work in business, though?

Well, let's say you want your audience to purchase your email marketing software. You might want to consider messaging that focuses on social proof to capture new customers.

Years ago, Constant Contact ran advertising tests in which it tested messaging focused on the hundreds of thousands of business customers it had at the time vs. other types of messaging, such as marketing ROI. The ads based on social proof won hands down. This led the company to update its home page and other marketing vehicles with social proof-centric messaging. The company then exploded with growth. Constant Contact was eventually acquired by Endurance International for an estimated $1.1 billion. I'm not saying that social proof was the only reason for the growth, but it certainly contributed.

Building trust with your website visitors is one of the most important ways you can increase the number of leads generated through your site. If they trust you more, they are far more likely to sign up for your mailing list, webinar, whitepaper, research report, free trial, etc. or to request to talk with your sales team.

Simple ways to include social proof in your website include the display of user-generated content, customer reviews and testimonials, awards that you've won, research and significant stats, number of customers you serve, industry leadership, etc.

There are a variety of ways you can start to build relationships and trust with site visitors. But social proof is one of the most powerful methods you can use and should be a part of every business website.

IP Detection

What's one of the most effective ways to generate leads from your website?

Without a doubt, it's using IP detection software such as Leadfeeder, Lead Forensics, or LiftCertain. It's the first thing I look at when starting my workday. I want to know exactly who has been on our website, what their intent is, and who we should reach out to.

Given the importance of website visitor identification, it's highly perplexing why so many B2B marketing teams don't have IP detection software installed in their website or simply choose not to review the data in the case it is installed. If ever there was a good reason to rethink your lead generation, making regular use of IP detection data would be a good place to start.

Think back to the first story in this chapter. It was through IP detection that our agency was able to capture a new lead from a company that simply wasn't filling out any of the forms in our website even though they kept coming back over and over again. The end result was that we started a conversation with them through contextually relevant outreach, and they ultimately became a good client.

Use IP detection software to ensure you know who is visiting your website so that you can customize your outreach, engagement, and conversations with them according to their interests. On top of this, by using IP detection software you can update your website in line with how you see your ideal audiences navigating your site and consuming its content.

If you use standard web analytics, you know what the aggregation of visitors are doing on your site. You can see the number of visitors, number of page views, the source of how they entered the site, etc. However, you don't know what each company, or in certain cases, specific individuals are doing while on your site.

Enter IP detection software, which reveals the company name and in the case the person is already in your database can also identify the person on your site. (Certain applications like Lift-Certain can identify individuals even if they are not in your database.)

An IP address is a unique string of numbers that identifies each computer using the Internet Protocol communicating over a network. If you know the IP address of a visitor to your website, it's often possible to identify the company from which they are coming, as well as unique computers within such company.

If you want to provide information, guidance, and support to your site visitors, knowing who they are is the first place to start. With IP detection software, you can see not only the company name, but also the source of their visit (e.g., Google search, advertisement, third-party website, etc.), along with the precise navigation route through your site, with time-on-page statistics for each page they landed on during the visit. By having access to IP detection data, you're essentially gathering first-party intent data.

If you see that they spent two minutes on pages related to one of your services, but only two seconds on a page related to a different service, bingo, you know what they are interested in and what they are not. Similarly, if you see them on half a dozen blog posts about account-based marketing (ABM) and video, you know how to spark a new conversation with them to which they'll likely be receptive.

IP detection is the difference between guessing what a brand might be interested in, and having conversations that immediately and directly get to the heart of what's of most interest to them. It's an intent data goldmine.

If you want your organization to be leads obsessed, IP detection software is a critical ingredient.

~

So, how can you up your game and make even better use of IP detection?

Custom filters.

Configuring custom filters is one of the smartest moves you can make. By setting up custom filters, you can group your site visitors and their associated analytics for more targeted outreach. For example, treat different site visitors differently, with different lead scores.

Some of your visitors are going to show buyer intent more than others even by just the pages they visit. This is why Stratabeat segments visitors within our IP detection software based on whether they were on our main services page, contact us page, or case study pages. We prioritize these individuals, as they are most likely ready to engage in a conversation about working together towards their marketing goals.

When we run ABM campaigns, we track visitors by the specific company.

Similarly, you can segment your site visitors by:

- Industry
- Location
- Source of the visit
- UTM code
- Company size
- Pages per visit
- Company name
- Etc.

Then, configure notifications so that your relevant team members are informed immediately or at least daily of new visitors meeting the custom filter requirements. By using a granular set of criteria to segment your visitors, you'll be much more efficient in reviewing them and conducting subsequent outreach to them.

Web Analytics

If you want more leads, you should be analyzing your web analytics on a regular basis and trying to identify opportunities for site improvements.

The biggest problem I see with web analytics usage, though, is lack of segmentation. Too many companies are looking at aggregate data instead of segmenting the data for more accurate analysis.

Rethink web analytics, and you'll get much more out of the data.

Take geography, for example. If your audience is in the United States, why would you include traffic from Brazil, Denmark, and India in your analysis? But that's what we see many marketing teams doing with their web analytics data. They take the default aggregate data and analyze the entire data set without any type of differentiation.

In a similar way, it's important to view your web analytics data based on the source of the traffic. It's one thing to treat all data as coming from the same intent, but typically that's not the case. For example, including traffic from your email campaigns together with traffic from organic and paid search doesn't make sense. You would expect their behavior on your site to differ, so why would you analyze the data together as if they were from the same source with the same intent requiring the same site experience? Yet, I see this all the time.

There are many types of segmentation available to you. Beyond geography and traffic source, you should be segmenting your desktop traffic from your mobile traffic. Similarly, segment new site visitors from returning visitors. On and on.

Be sure to configure your web analytics so that you're segmenting the data in as many ways as is useful to your marketing. Otherwise, you're not dealing with clean, reliable data, and the subsequent updates you make to your website may actually hurt your lead gen efforts, not help them.

Behavioral Analytics

When analyzing Google Analytics or other web analytics data for a web page, you're looking at high-level results for the page as a whole. What I want you to do is rethink your analytics. To gain deeper, more valuable insights, use *behavioral analytics*.

Too many marketers are not capitalizing on behavioral analytics, or worse, don't even know about it. I've spoken at industry conferences around the U.S. through the years, and it always astounds me when I ask the audience if they are using behavioral analytics, and typically only five to 10 percent of the audience affirms in the positive.

How in the world can this be? It leads me to believe that the majority of marketers need to rethink how they are measuring the performance of their website.

With behavioral analytics, you'll uncover not only where your site visitors are from and where they go in your site, but also what they do specifically within each page. Discover exactly where site visitors are spending the most time on the page, moving their cursor, scrolling, hovering, clicking, and focusing their attention. Based on this data, you'll be able to make pinpoint adjustments to drive conversion rates and leads higher.

For example, in Stratabeat's blog, we often review behavioral analytics to see within an individual post what the reader is most interested in on the page. We can see which CTAs they are viewing, and which they never see. We can also see where they might be abandoning the post. We can then adjust the post accordingly for greater engagement, increased conversions, and an optimum experience.

In one post about browser testing tools, for instance, we had noticed that readers were skipping over one of the tools towards the top of the page but were clicking a high percentage of the time on the tool at the bottom of the list. So, we adjusted the ordering of the tools, bringing the more popular tool towards the top. Sure enough, with more people seeing the popular tool, time-on-page and clicks increased substantially. Even the scroll rate improved. Across all the metrics we reviewed, the post's performance improved, delivering a better user experience.

For an enterprise software client, through the use of behavioral analytics we noticed that approximately half of the visitors to the product suite page (the most important page in the entire site) abandoned the page after only the first component of the suite. In other words, roughly half of the visitors interested in checking out their software never saw the two other components making up the product suite. Well, I can tell you that if a site visitor never sees two-thirds of the value of what you're selling, you're probably not going to generate many leads.

And sure enough, the poor page construction was having a negative impact on this software company's leads. With a newly designed page that brought the other two components to the top of the page and added all components individually to the top navigation, leads increased.

Typical web analytics packages would never reveal this type of information to you. This is why it's so critical for you to layer in behavioral analysis, beyond web analytics alone.

Session Recordings

Using behavioral analytics software, you can see much more than the data. You can also view actual recordings of your site visitors' sessions through your website. This type of qualitative analysis helps you go beyond the quantitative insights you glean from your web and behavioral analytics. It helps you to solve costly user experience frustrations and recover at-risk conversions.

With session recordings, you can see exactly how they move through each page during their site visit. You can see where they slow down and focus their attention. You can see what's working well and generating leads within your website. Alternatively, you can see where they breeze through it without actually reading the content, skipping to the next page in their journey. You can also view where there's friction in the site experience, when they become frustrated, confused, or lose interest.

Web analytics tells you the "what" of your site visitors' experience. Video replays uncover the "why".

For example, for a financial services website, our agency had developed an interactive wizard for site visitors. Within the wizard was a calendar feature for date selection. We felt that the feature made it extremely easy for site visitors to select the date and move on to the next question.

However, in looking at the session recordings, we noticed that a number of site visitors were trying to manually enter the date instead of simply selecting the date by using the tool. This was counterintuitive, as the tool made date selection incredibly easy to do. Yet, some site visitors were trying over and over to enter the date manually, even though manual entry would be more effort on their part.

When we noticed this, we immediately updated the tool to enable manual date entry as an option. Site visitors could either use the tool for easy date selection, or they could enter the date manually in any format they preferred.

The new approach led to an increase in conversion rate of wizard completions, with each one being a new lead.

If we had relied solely on web analytics or even quantitative behavioral analytics, we never would have been able to identify the problem. With *session recordings*, it became immediately apparent, and we were able to make the corrective adjustments to the process and improve lead generation.

Watching video recordings takes time. To ensure you're capitalizing on the videos while using your time efficiently, use friction scores or other negative metrics from your behavioral analytics software to help you identify trouble spots in your website. Then, review those videos first.

And be sure to filter the videos by geography. As mentioned earlier, you want to analyze only those site visitors who are in your actual target geographic regions. You'll also want to segment your analysis for desktop vs. mobile and for first-time visitors compared to returning visitors. Website navigational behavior can be significantly different on desktop compared to mobile, and whereas first time visitors are trying to find things on your site, returning visitors often tend to know exactly where to go.

Personalization

Website personalization is another area of opportunity for you to increase leads from your website, yet many companies are not doing any personalization. There are many tools available that can enable you to personalize your web pages, ranging from marketing automation platforms to IP detection software to dedicated personalization tools.

The key is not the specific tool you use, but how you implement personalization in your site.

When Meagen Eisenberg (introduced in the prior chapter) was CMO at MongoDB, she and her team achieved remarkable results through website personalization. By personalizing the site experience through a variety of tools, the website went from 100 to 7,500 downloads per week in support of the company's enterprise products within two and half years. And that was only the gated results. When they ungated the content, they achieved over 30,000 weekly downloads. Powerful stuff!

Keep in mind that any page in your website can be personalized. You can personalize the actual messaging they see on the page, or the imagery, or the offers and CTAs you present to them. What you want to decide is on the strategic ways in which you can personalize experiences that will make a real difference in the site experience of your visitors.

Low-hanging fruit for personalization is to personalize web pages for those already in your CRM database. You can do this by tagging your contacts according to their audience segment, contact source, geographic location, expressed interest, or various other categories. You can use any tag — whether it's based on interest, sentiment, or engagement — to personalize text, images, and CTAs.

For example, if you conduct ABM campaigns, then personalizing the landing pages or even the pages within your main site for those specific companies makes a lot of sense. After all, you want to deliver as customized an experience as possible for your most valuable target audience members. And this approach is not limited to ABM.

You could test it with various types of campaigns, aligning the campaign messaging with what's on the destination web pages.

If you're a B2B marketer with a narrowly defined target market, that would be another great opportunity for personalizing the pages that site visitors see based on the company visiting your site.

Another way that you can use personalization is through the use of interactive wizards or surveys. These types of tools are useful in capturing further details about your site visitors that can be used for further segmentation and personalization. If it's clear through the use of a wizard or survey that they are interested in a specific topic, product, or solution, then take them to a web page that delivers that to them as a next step.

And if you just want to keep it simple, you can still achieve meaningful customization per audience segment without dynamic content. An easy one is to segment by target industry. In doing so, you can funnel your visitors to an area of your site that speaks to their specific industry challenges and needs, together with content, case studies, testimonials, downloads, CTAs, etc. that are specific to their industry. Or follow this same approach, but with segmentation based on department or role at the company. Simple personalization can be powerful. Walk before you run.

Personalization not only leads to increased time-on-site and a better user experience, but it also increases your conversion rates. Although many businesses have yet to implement any kind of personalization on their website, it can improve your site performance significantly.

Rethink your website and explore how you might be able to inject a bit of personalization.

Marketing Automation

Helping marketers to be more efficient, marketing automation is the process of using software to automate certain marketing processes and tasks. The main objective is to streamline and scale lead management and other marketing activities. Marketing automation is like having an additional employee on your marketing team!

Yet, there are countless B2B websites that are not capitalizing on the major benefits of marketing automation.

The automation is most often integrated with a CRM system and used to help nurture leads. The software is also used to automate and personalize site content and messaging.

Given that repetitive tasks only slow you down and that customization only helps to improve results, it behooves any marketing organization to utilize marketing automation.

You can use the software to help you track and score leads, communicate through email, and to customize content on your site. If you segment your audience, then marketing automation takes on a more robust and effective role.

AND IF YOU want to take things to an entirely new level, you should rethink your marketing by executing marketing automation via behavioral segmentation.

It's one thing to initiate an automated email campaign to someone who downloaded a whitepaper, but without further insight you run the risk of not understanding their intent and continually marketing to them misaligned with their interests and needs.

Behavioral segmentation is your answer to better, more effective marketing. Use behavioral segmentation to not only make more sophisticated use of your marketing automation sequences, but to also resonate more deeply and to engage with your audience more effectively.

Behavioral segmentation categorizes your audience according to the behavioral patterns they exhibit as they interact with your brand. This type of segmentation looks at the digital body language of your site visitors. It examines where the experience is enjoyable and aligned with their intent, and where friction enters the process and forces them to abandon your brand. Behavioral segmentation responds to the actions your audience takes and evolves over the lifespan of the prospect.

There are various types of behavioral segmentation for you to consider. Start with one or two, and then expand from there.

For B2B marketers, these are some of the most common types:

- **Based on Content Consumed** — If one of your site visitors is consuming information about SEO, they are clearly different from those reading about conversion

optimization while on your site. Similarly, if they visit your Product A page and another visits your Product B page instead, they clearly have different problems to solve and should be targeted differently.
- **Based on Website Navigation** — If you've recognized that your top prospects go from your home page to your services page to your case studies pages, you can target them differently than those who read a blog post but never visited your services page (and therefore have shown a very different level of buyer intent).
- **Based on Level of Engagement** — Someone who comes to your site and reads one page is displaying quite different behavior than someone who has consumed more than five pages, and then comes again the following day for another five pages. Similarly, someone who visits once, downloads a whitepaper, and never visits again, is demonstrating different behavior than someone who has repeatedly taken an action in your website, whether downloading content, signing up for webinars, requesting a demo, or watching your videos, etc.
- **Based on Purchasing Behavior** — If you're a B2B business that enables a purchase right on your site (think SaaS), you can also segment your audience based on their purchasing behavior. For example, someone who signs up for a freemium account is different from other purchasers who have made a monetary commitment.

Let's say two individuals download your whitepaper. They both receive the autoresponder, click the link and check it out.

They both return to your site, but the paths they take are quite different. One looks at Product A, while the other Product B. One looks at certain case studies, the other different case studies. One looks at certain blog posts, the other different posts.

Using these additional behavioral signals you can send more finely-tuned customized emails or even split your automation altogether. From there, you can repeat the process as many times as makes sense.

In other words, everyone in your database should have been put through not one segmentation filter, but at least two or more. The deeper segmentation opens up a multitude of options for connecting with your audience members in more meaningful ways.

Behavioral segmentation is nothing short of a game changer if you want significantly greater results from your marketing.

A/B Testing

Too many teams approach their website as "set it and forget it".

Ahhhhhhhh. It's enough to drive a marketer bananas!

If you're not conducting A/B tests (or multivariate tests if you have sufficient traffic), you're most certainly missing out on higher performance from your website. An A/B test shows two different versions of a site element to your site visitors so that a certain percentage of visitors see one version and other visitors see the other version. It's an efficient and effective way to have your audience validate what works best in your website.

To gain more value out of your A/B testing, document your hypothesis prior to launching each test. This will help you glean more specific, usable insight from your tests.

In addition, set up a testing plan. Don't just start testing site elements randomly. A longer-term plan ensures that your testing will be methodical and cover different aspects of your site in a logical order.

Even with deciding which tests to conduct, be deliberate. I recommend assessing each testing idea using a matrix (similar to what we walked through earlier) that evaluates:

- Speed
- Ease
- Cost
- Potential Revenue
- Potential Overall ROI or Impact

And here's the thing. Many marketers aren't even aware of many of the ways that you can conduct A/B testing.

With conversion optimization software, you can test just about any aspect of your website. Your messaging, copy length, images, video, CTAs, etc. Want to test displaying a video compared with a bullet list? No problem. Even with just a CTA button alone, you can test the button color, text, hover effect, shape, and size.

For greater impact to your business, track across the entire funnel with A/B tests at various steps along the way.

If you want to amp up your testing even further, you can set up A/B tests based on your site visitors' behavior. For example, present different offers and CTAs based on the pages they visit or what they click on, or how long they are on a page, how far they scroll down a page, or if they are leaving your website, etc.

You can A/B test offers and CTAs to those who take a certain action within your site and then remain on your site. Similarly, you can test offers and CTAs to those who left your site and then returned at another time.

In other words, fine tune your CTAs to match their digital body language, and you'll achieve new heights with your site performance.

So, if you're not conducting A/B tests in your website, you should rethink what you're doing and start a methodical, ongoing testing program. Instead of viewing your site as a static platform, treat it as a strategic petri dish for a precision-engineered, fine-tuned website.

Chapter Summary

If you want your website to be a lead generation engine, then rethink the possibilities. From IP detection to session video recordings to marketing automation, are you doing all that you should in order to maximize your site leads?

- Is your website audience-centric and full of value for them? Are you using "you" language throughout the site?
- Have you defined your audience segments and personas, and then mapped the associated customer journeys?
- When they hit your site, do you know the specific questions running through their minds?
- What type of voice of the customer (VoC) activities are you engaged in to try to understand your audience more deeply?
- What's your hook? Is it being clearly articulated in your site?
- Your site visitors are judging your website within

milliseconds upon arrival. Is your site delivering high cognitive fluency, leading to a better brand touchpoint?
- Be sure to map your conversion funnels and optimize your landing pages.
- Use multiple CTAs on a page and test various types of CTAs. To improve performance even further, add behaviorally-triggered CTAs.
- How can you add more social proof to your site to build trust with site visitors?
- Use IP detection software to uncover which companies are visiting your website. Then conduct outreach based on the pages and content they consumed during their visit. Do this every day!
- Go beyond web analytics. Use behavioral analytics and session recordings to see their digital body language and ensure their visits are frictionless and leading to great experiences.
- How are you personalizing the site experience?
- Using marketing automation software is like having an extra employee. Are you capitalizing on the opportunity and turbocharging your website/marketing performance?
- For your many website initiatives, remember to test, test, and then test some more.

3

SEO AND CONTENT MARKETING

Once you've transformed your website into a lead generation platform, you should focus on driving qualified traffic to your site.

Two of my favorite ways to do this are SEO and content marketing. The two go hand-in-hand in attracting highly qualified traffic to your website, driving new leads, and fueling growth.

Beyond audience insight, SEO should be used for content planning and attracting the right traffic. Organic Google rankings guide individuals to the very content they seek at the precise time they are looking for it. SEO helps you to expand your reach, fill your funnel, and multiply your brand touchpoints.

But that's not all SEO achieves. In neuroscience, the Mere Exposure Effect is a recognized phenomenon whereby the more often people are exposed to something, the more they like it. Any brand that achieves strong organic visibility (and therefore familiarity) in Google capitalizes on the Mere Exposure Effect and winds up with more people favoring their brand subconsciously. That subconscious preference benefits your brand as those audience members continue through the customer journey, consider their options, and make purchase decisions.

Content marketing serves a complementary purpose to SEO. It should answer their questions, solve their problems, help them achieve their goals, establish trust, differentiate your brand, fuel word of mouth, and build brand love with the audience. It should also help you drive a great number of leads in the process.

The combination of SEO and content is a crazy effective lead generation engine for your business. What's truly magical about them is that once you achieve the flywheel effect, the results compound over time.

I mean, seriously, what other marketing compounds over time?

For one of Stratabeat's recently onboarded accounts, our client went from zero organic, inbound leads prior to engaging with us to being so inundated with leads that they could barely keep up. Another client needed to hire 200 additional employees within two years, growing 5X in the process, to support their growth. This is the power of SEO and content.

However, many marketing teams fumble the ball when it comes to SEO and content marketing. Countless companies spend years at it, with little to no results. Many marketers simply walk away, mistakenly feeling that it's impossible to break through and achieve success.

According to Content Marketing Institute's and MarketingProfs' *12th Annual Content Marketing Benchmarks, Budgets, and Trends: Insights for 2022* report, 72 percent of the most successful content marketers generate leads from their content marketing initiatives while only 36 percent of laggards are able to make the same claim.[13]

Unfortunately, most companies are laggards when it comes to content marketing. There's so much poorly executed SEO and mediocre content out there, it's shocking.

There's a great deal of untapped opportunity. Many marketing teams are treading water. They continually crank out content, yet never see any results from it.

Instead, if you want to achieve massive results from your organic marketing, rethink how you're creating optimized content. And that's what I'm going to walk you through in this chapter of the book. I've been doing SEO for 16 years. I've seen some strategies work very effectively, and I've seen others with zero ROI. I'm going to share only the stuff I know to be true and useful with you.

Before we get into the details, a word of warning. Although Stratabeat uses many SEO and content marketing technologies, for the most part I'm not going to review specific tools here. The tools on the market are evolving quickly, and new tools are entering the market all the time.

In order to keep the advice evergreen, I'm going to focus on the strategies you need to achieve better organic search and content results on an ongoing basis. That way, you can increase your leads from this chapter regardless of when you're reading it.

When $300 Million Can't Drive Organic Growth

At the time of this writing, there are more than 8 billion Google searches daily. And various studies through the years have shown that the majority of individuals click on the organic listings in the Google search results pages, far more than click on the paid advertisements. If you want to maximize traffic to your website, organic search is the answer.

Yet, even so, our agency runs across many companies that have no idea how to capitalize on SEO or content to drive business growth when we first meet them. Sometimes they just simply ignore these growth drivers. Other times, they are actively engaged in these activities, yet producing no results for the business. Even companies with hundreds of millions of venture capital dollars often falter when it comes to SEO and content.

Why is this such a pervasive problem?

I believe the following experience illustrates the shortsightedness of many marketing teams. It reveals the lack of willingness of some groups to work hard, honestly assess the weaknesses of their prior approaches, and do what it really takes to earn consistently high Google rankings and a strong flow of organic traffic.

One company with more than $300 million in investments from VCs, for example, requested that our agency help them optimize their blog and the video content in their YouTube channel.

First, let's talk about their blog. It was almost invisible in Google. This was partly due to content that wasn't optimized to any topics or keywords for which the audience was searching. It was also partly due to a web hosting platform that resulted in a page load speed slower than molasses. Stratabeat outlined an SEO plan to transform their blog, including a migration to a lightning-fast hosting infrastructure.

Nah, that was too much work in their eyes. So, the blog continues to this day to generate close to zero organic views.

OK, it wasn't going to happen with the blog, but we were still optimistic about the YouTube videos. The existing channel was badly lacking views when we first audited it.

After reviewing their YouTube account, our answer back to them was that they didn't have a single video worth optimizing.

Instead, they needed to completely rethink the types of content to add to YouTube in order to gain viewers, captivate them, and generate real business ROI. They needed to blow up their existing library of videos. They needed to change their approach from one of talking about themselves to one that was far more customer-centric. From one that was accurate yet boring, to one that was captivating and engaging. From one that ignored analytics to one that optimized based on the data for continually greater performance.

We provided them with a list of new videos to develop to captivate their audience in YouTube. We were super excited to start storyboarding the videos. They were going to be awesome. We couldn't wait.

But...

The $300 million company refused. They felt that our approach was too much work. Instead, they tried "optimizing" their existing library of videos by themselves and didn't create any of the types of more engaging, more customer-centric content that we were recommending.

The result?

A big thud. Absolutely no change in viewership of their videos. What they had on their hands was a collection of *optimized mediocrity*. And still very few video views.

To this day, their YouTube channel is a disaster. Of the last 20 videos published in their YouTube channel at the time of this writing, 90 percent have fewer than 25 total views and none of the videos have even 165 views. Ouch!

Why do companies do this? Especially a company with $300 million in the bank. Yet, this type of random approach is not uncommon.

If you're struggling with your SEO and content as so many companies are today, I ask you to rethink everything you know about these marketing vehicles and to reimagine how they can contribute to your growth.

Powerful Traffic Growth through SEO

So, clearly there's a right way to optimize content, and there are approaches where you'll be merely running around in circles awash in frustration.

It's time to massively increase your traffic and leads through SEO and content. Not just any old SEO and content. You're going to transform your site through a sophisticated framework. Plus, you're going to stack multiple SEO and content marketing strategies for bigger gains.

Let's start by looking at an example where a company absolutely crushed it. Ahrefs is a true organic growth story. There's a lot to learn from their approach to SEO and content.

When Tim Soulo, Ahrefs' CMO, arrived at the SEO platform company, the blog was attracting approximately 15,000 visitors a month. This was with three new blog posts weekly. The problem was, traffic had hit a plateau. They just couldn't generate new traffic growth no matter what they tried.

Three years later, Soulo and his team achieved 1,136 percent traffic growth.[14] And during two of those years it was with two posts per week and one of those years with merely one post weekly.

The results from the blog were not limited to traffic. Annual recurring revenue (ARR) climbed at a similar 10X clip in parallel.

Less output, 10X the results. Sweet!

So, how did they do it?

They focused exclusively on long-term SEO. Unlike so many others in the industry, they completely ignored hot topics or the latest news from Google. Instead, the Ahrefs team looked at topics that could deliver organic traffic not only today, but also tomorrow, the next month, the next year, and the next few years. By taking this approach, each blog post would be an investment with ongoing returns for years to come. With a solid blog library built in this way, you get a flood of ongoing traffic that keeps flowing like a river. (Yet, how often do you see companies without any clear blogging strategy or direction?)

In addition, they went all-in on long-form posts. If you look at their blog, most of their posts are over 2,500 words. Some are over 4,000 words. (Yet, how often do you see companies with 700-word fluff pieces without any meat to the content?)

Another aspect of their approach that's highly effective is the use of data for proprietary information and insight. In one study, Ahrefs reviewed 3 million web pages in researching the number of keywords for which a single page could rank. In another study, the company looked at 2 million web pages to identify the percentage of online content that doesn't attract any organic traffic. (Yet, how often do you see companies without any original insight that simply regurgitate topics that have been covered by hundreds of other blogs?)

Ahrefs also made their posts highly actionable. They took the reader step-by-step through processes to achieve their optimization objectives and tackle challenges. They included many screenshots in their posts so that it would be easy for readers to take immediate action without the need for further support. (Yet, how often do you see companies that talk at a 10,000-foot view, and never deliver any granular, actionable advice?)

In addition, they removed all posts that were not delivering traffic, which resulted in more than half of the existing posts being eliminated within three years. That's right, they deleted the majority of their blog posts. By pruning the library of content and removing the low-traffic noise, Ahrefs was able to help Google understand the exact topics on which they were authoritative. (Yet, how often do you see companies maintain non-performing posts for years and years?)

Other tactics by Ahrefs?

They focused on only topics with business potential. In other words, the intent behind the search would need to indicate a good fit for purchasing an Ahrefs subscription. Very straightforward. Blog post titles such as "Canonical Tags: A Simple Guide for Beginners", "How To Do Keyword Research for SEO — Ahrefs' Guide", and "13 Best Link Building Tools (for Building AMAZING Links)." In Soulo's own words, they have looked to publish posts where the Ahrefs product is helpful or even essential.

(Yet, time and time again you see blog post topics on B2B sites around the web that are irrelevant and are useless for lead generation. Why is it that when a content team has a mandate to generate more blog traffic, tying everything back to business results is so commonly ignored?)

Let's look at another example of growth through SEO and content.

Stratabeat is a marketing agency. We help clients increase organic traffic through optimized content. We recently helped a client achieve 6,112 percent organic blog page view growth in three years.

What was the key to success?

There were actually several keys…

First, although it might sound counterintuitive, we guided the client through a complete redesign of their website. If you want amazing SEO results, then make sure your website is built correctly. From rethinking the site taxonomy to the words on the page, we changed almost everything about our client's website. We transformed the messaging to speak to the audience's goals and objectives. Although the client was targeting the Fortune 500, the prior website made them look amateurish at best. The new website made Fortune 500 visitors feel at home, with appropriate messaging, case studies, and content.

Starting with a strong brand and a strong website that appeals to the target audience is important to organic growth success. Always start there!

Second, we focused on building SEO topic clusters, which are a hub-and-spoke model of content, centered on specific topic areas. I go into detail on this content development structure later in this chapter, and I'll tell you that it's an extremely powerful approach to winning more organic search rankings and traffic.

Third, we prioritized long-form content. Most posts are approximately 3,000 words in length, while others are 4K or 5K. If the average word count on Google page one for a target keyword was 3,000, we'd make sure we beat it. If the average was 3,500, we'd beat it. If the average was 4,000, we'd beat it. Not with fluff. Rather, we would write more by diving deeper into the topic and overwhelming the reader with a tsunami of value. Whereas most marketers would think it insane, we typically would spend 10-15 hours on a single post. So, it was a combination of both long-form content and extremely high-quality content.

Fourth, we focused on "related keywords" just as much as the core target keyword. With SEO, you typically define a single primary keyword, and that's the keyword on which you want the content piece to rank in Google. Our efforts went further by including a wide range of related keywords, words that appear throughout the listings on Google page one and keywords for which the Google page one listing is also ranking at the top of Google.

Fifth, we made the content come alive with many examples, stories, case studies, research, statistics, videos, screenshots, etc. By not only *telling* readers what they should know, but also *showing* them real-world examples, the content was more engaging and led to more online sharing and more inbound links from other websites. Too often, this aspect of SEO is completely ignored, but great content will significantly outperform mediocre content when all else is equal. Actually, I believe that this was one of the secrets to achieving 6,112 percent growth for our client. The effort was focused not only on optimizing the content, but also on creating an amazing experience for the reader.

In addition, the client understands SEO. Having an entire team totally bought-in, synchronized, and completely focused on optimized content helps more than you might think.

Thrilling Your Audience AND Generating Incredible Marketing Results

When you create content for your brand, be sure to make amazing content that your target audience will be thrilled to read (or at the very least will find extremely useful). Remember, there's a ton of crappy content out there. Don't add to it. Instead, help your audience to achieve their objectives, solve their problems, eliminate pain, or entertain them.

It's as simple as that.

The reason why Ahrefs had such success with their blog is because the content was not only high quality but it was also exactly what their target audiences wanted in learning to eliminate specific challenges. Plus, the blog was effectively optimized so that many new audience members could easily find it in Google.

If you look at those who are crushing it in Google, they are often thrilling a narrow, targeted audience. Think of the online database platform Airtable. The templates section of their website is an effective onramp for using their software. The templates save their users hours that they would otherwise spend building their own templates and workspaces. By focusing so extensively on building a library of templates, they are attracting the exact audience who would find their database solution highly useful. The template pages alone rank on Google page one for more than 1,600 keywords.

Accenture is another example. They aim to thrill their audience with blog content customized to a range of different markets and topics. Instead of hosting just one blog, they publish 15 industry blogs (e.g., banking, capital markets, energy) and 13 topical blogs (e.g., Accenture research, blockchain, interactive insights). By pumping out content that's specific to many different industries and topics, they are able to connect more deeply with a wider range of segments. This has helped Accenture to rank on Google page one for tens of thousands of keywords.

So, you can see, there are various ways to thrill your audience with content. You don't need to fit into a cookie-cutter mold. No matter how you do it, remember to thrill your audience when you're creating content for them and not to focus solely on Google.

Tree Ring Multiplier Strategy

If you're looking for higher organic traffic results, I recommend you start with the Tree Ring Multiplier Strategy.

One of the fastest ways to gain organic search rankings is to target areas where you already have a foothold, and to focus, augment, and amplify your efforts from there. In other words, if you already are ranking on Google page one for a keyword or a few keywords, you should target related, adjacent long-tail keywords.

Think of it this way. Let's say you're a phenom in tennis. You're the second coming of Serena Williams. Because you're so strong in tennis, it should be relatively easy for you to start playing squash, racquetball, or even ping pong. Because you're so strong in tennis, it wouldn't be long before you were crushing the competition in all these *related* sports.

Now let's flip the analogy a bit. If you tried to go from tennis to rock climbing or football, that would probably be significantly more difficult. In fact, you could be a complete failure.

This is almost precisely what happened to Michael Jordan when he tried to switch from playing basketball to baseball. He is, arguably, the greatest basketball player of all time, but on the baseball diamond, he was mediocre.

Now, let's take this principle of related proximity and use it to attain better Google rankings, faster and easier.

The first step in this process is to determine your keywords already ranking on Google page one.

Then, determine the ones that have the greatest impact on your business. Define a set of related keywords and start building content around them, linking among the different content pieces. Start developing an ecosystem of related keywords.

Google already sees you as an authority for your primary keyword. They rank you on page one, which indicates that you're trustworthy and authoritative in Google's eyes.

Capitalize on this! Go beyond keyword success to achieve topical success, and greatly expand your rankings and organic traffic in the process.

How do you find "related keywords" to determine complementary topics to write about?

There are multiple ways to do this. For example, let's say that you currently rank on Google page one for "business loan" and you're looking to expand your traction from that centerpoint. Follow these steps:

- Use a keyword research tool such as Ahrefs or Semrush. Enter "business loan" and review the related keywords displayed by the tool. This is a fast way to uncover hundreds of keyword ideas.

- Check the options that appear in the drop-down menu in the Google search bar as you type "business loan". Then, type "business loan a" and see what pops up in the drop-down menu. After that, try "business loan b", "business loan c", "business loan d", etc. and continue through the alphabet. You'd be surprised how many new, related keywords you can quickly uncover this way.
- Check Google's Related Searches at the bottom of the Google search results page when you search for "business loan".
- Check the People Also Ask box on the Google search results page, if one is displayed.
- Dig deeper into the other Google page one rankings for "business loan" to discover additional keywords for which they are ranking on page one. For example, take the top Google organic result for "business loan" and use a tool such as Ahrefs or Semrush to identify other keywords for which the page is also ranking on Google page one.
- Log into Google Search Console and review the related queries listed under "Performance" for which your site is already appearing in the search results.
- Go to a few industry publications and blogs. Review articles or posts related to "business loan", and see what other, related topics, phrases, and keywords you find.
- Go to YouTube, and similarly explore the top videos for a search on "business loan" to uncover related topics and phrases.
- Take notes from your conversations with customers and prospects. What are they talking about? How do they articulate their thoughts?

Google Page Two and Page Three

Another area to focus on early in your SEO initiatives is on Google page two and page three. If you're already ranking on Google page one for a target keyword, then you have incremental opportunities for better positioning. However, if you move a ranking from page two or three to Google page one, you're more likely to achieve a massive increase in traffic from that keyword.

Given that the keyword is already generating a ranking on page two or three means that Google identifies your site as an authority to some degree on the keyword already. And so in that sense this is lower hanging fruit for your SEO efforts.

The overall work required to push a page two or three ranking onto Google page one is much lower than trying to get a non-ranking keyword even onto page two or three. But the traffic that you can expect to generate through a page one ranking is always going to be much greater than one that's outside of the first page of search results.

Once you start making progress with your Google organic rankings through the Tree Ring Multiplier Strategy described above, attacking your Google page two and three rankings is one of the fastest ways to see additional SEO progress.

How do you improve your rankings currently on page two and three? The first thing you should do is make sure that your content truly rocks. Make it better than anything on Google page one. Then, build out related content, as you would with the Tree Ring Multiplier Strategy. This sends a signal to Google that your website focuses on these topics. Then, add links among the related content and those pages ranking on page two and three. This further communicates to Google that you have deep, inter-related content on the topic. And finally, identify sites that are already linking to the content on Google page one for those keywords and conduct outreach to see if they would want to link to your content, as well. If your content is highly complementary to anything already ranking on Google page one, two, or three, by all means seek a link from those websites, as well.

Many marketers believe that you should simply go after keywords with the highest search volume. That's just not the case. Be more strategic and selective. Start with low-hanging fruit and build an SEO moat for your business. With SEO, it really is a case of a rising tide lifting all boats. With strong success in narrow, focused topic areas, you gain invaluable trust from Google, and this trust then translates into easier rankings for anything else you target that's related to your page one rankings.

From there, it will be far faster and far easier to expand your Google rankings. And when you see a new batch of keywords on page two and three, you get to focus on them just as you did initially. The cycle repeats itself over and over. This is an ongoing process that enables you to keep moving search results from page two and three to page one, as part of a continuous process.

Different Content for Different Roles

With SEO, you'll often hear advice that you should select a keyword and then simply optimize a piece of content for that keyword. Then, it's on to the next keyword.

However, I would argue that B2B is more complex than that.

You need to completely rethink how you approach optimized content if you seriously want to move your audience towards an actual sale.

B2B business is unique in that a single sale often involves multiple team members over a long time period. For example, you have your decision maker, of course. But then there's often an influencer, a financial decision maker, a business user, a technical lead, etc. The different buyer roles contribute to the conversation in different ways at different times through the decision-making process.

Each role has different questions they need to answer in order to contribute effectively to the group. This covers everything from problem identification to solution exploration, requirements and key factors gathering, options definition, risk mitigation, and solution/seller selection. In many cases, online research can take half of the team's time spent in the buying journey, meaning less time actually talking with you and your team.

Be sure to write optimized content for the different roles.

If you're blindly just writing for the ultimate decision maker, you're likely going to fall short and not even realize it.

Let's go back to our "business loan" keyword example and see what we need to do. The keyword "business loan" is extremely broad. If we look at the People Also Ask questions in Google along with other questions being asked online, we see multiple angles into the intent of different team members.

For example, an executive may be asking:

- How to get a $100,000 business loan?
- How to use business loans to grow a business?
- What are smart ways to use a business loan?

- How to make a business loan go as far as possible?
- How to get the lowest interest rate on a business loan?

In contrast, the person tasked with exploring business loan options may be asking:

- What are business loan options?
- What are the best business loans?
- What is the minimum amount for a business loan?
- Which type of loan is best for a small business?
- What is the easiest SBA loan to get?
- Etc.

In this way, we can take a deeper dive into the psychology of each individual on the team and see things from their perspective. What role do they play on the team? What are they most concerned about? What answers do they need to contribute during team discussions?

Looking at it from each angle enables you to see the actual purchase process more holistically (and realistically). Instead of seeing optimized content as something that is tied to merely a single keyword, you instead see the process, personalities, and perspectives. This gives you keen insight for developing richer, more valuable content that they are more likely to value.

Yet, look at how many SEO and content teams work. Very little time is spent (if any) identifying content for different roles in the buying decision.

Think differently. Create content differently. Strive to win over the entire buying team, and watch your conversion rates increase.

Different Content for Different Steps in the Journey

Similarly, develop different content pieces for the various steps in the buyer journey. It's critical that you're supplying them with the right information at each stage of each journey.

For example, you might want to create broad content for when they first realize they have a question and start looking for answers. Each content piece should address the question at hand, but should ideally also guide them to the next step in their journey. In this way, you build trust and start a relationship with them.

When they're on your website, it's a similar story. You want to map the various funnels of how they are navigating your site. If you're not sure, you can check your web analytics as well as your behavioral analytics. Then, once the funnels are clear, spend the time optimizing them with the precise information they need to answer the questions going through their minds and guiding them to the next step.

Going deeper, think of the content you'll need once you make your offer. And remember, the offer is not necessarily a transaction. Often with B2B the offer is focused on lead generation through a download, webinar, product demo, subscription, audit, consultation, etc.

Zooming in, someone at the beginning of their journey may be satisfied with a number of informative blog posts. As they consume information on your website, they may find a deeper-dive webinar to be helpful in advancing along their journey. Yet, when they are trying to make a final decision, they might find an ROI calculator or a competitor matrix much more valuable.

Create content strategically. Align your content with their journey, and you'll build a stronger pipeline and close more deals.

Aligning with Search Intent

Let's talk about search intent. I cannot stress the importance of this enough.

Too many marketers aim to get onto Google page one without a clear idea as to what the individual is actually looking for. Sure, they typed the keyword into Google. But I mean, do you understand the specific type of content that's going to satisfy their search and is also what Google is looking to place on the first page of search results?

I'll give you an example. If someone searches for "business loan", they are probably looking for information about how to apply and secure a loan.

However, if they instead type "best business loans", then they are instead looking for a list of different options and a review or evaluation of the best ones.

If they query "best business loans for startups", then they want that list to include only options for those just starting out.

"Types of business loans" better include an explanation of each type of loan, "paypal business loan" needs to focus entirely on PayPal's fixed-term loan offering, and "how to get a million dollar business loan" needs to speak to the unique steps involved in securing a seven-figure loan specifically.

If your content doesn't align with the specific intent of the person making the query, then Google is likely not going to consider your content as highly relevant. Worse, even if you somehow did achieve a high Google ranking, there's going to be a great deal of disappointment on the part of the searcher when they realize your content doesn't satisfy their search intent. If they are not converting and you're not seeing any business value from a keyword ranking, then what's the point?

As an agency owner, I've met countless marketing teams through the years. It's surprising how many believe that just targeting a few broad-based keywords is their idea of SEO.

That's not how it works. At all.

For every keyword, investigate the underlying intent, and then do everything possible to provide the most valuable information in line with such intent.

How does Stratabeat identify the search intent of a query? We scrape and then analyze all of the data from Google page one. I literally mean *everything* on page one. This includes the titles, meta descriptions, headers, common words being used, questions being asked, related searches, etc. Armed with the actual data from Google, we can easily uncover the search intent from Google's perspective. From there, we reverse engineer the precise content that will match search intent while providing even greater value to readers than what's currently on Google page one.

YOU CAN ALSO EXAMINE search intent at a website level. In other words, what strongly resonates in general with a site's visitors overall?

For example, Stratabeat conducted an analysis for a website dedicated to business advice and found that the information that resonated most was quick-hitting, how-to listicles.

Why? Because business owners don't have time for wordy introductions or fluff pieces. They need quick-hitting directions to get stuff done and move the needle fast. So, we pounded out many listicles on the topics in which they were most interested and increased organic traffic to the site by more than 100,000 monthly organic visitors.

Align with intent, and drive massive traffic gains.

LET'S return to the online database platform Airtable to see how they align with audience intent.

Airtable thought through their content from the perspective of their audience. Sure, they have a blog, but that's not where they focus their energies and resources.

Instead, as mentioned earlier, Airtable goes all out on providing templates to its audience. This is brilliant, as it provides the very tools that will help new customers become actual users of their solution. It helps them to make useful databases and apps faster, making it more likely they'll stick with the platform.

In total, Airtable offers more than 300 templates across 21 categories in its template library. Beyond the templates section of the website, Airtable also offers what's called the "Universe", where users can upload Airtable creations of their own for others to use.

At the time of this writing, Airtable ranks on Google page one and two for more than 1,400 phrases that include the word "template". These phrases are searched in Google in the U.S. more than 160,000 times monthly, translating into visibility on more than 1.92 million annual searches for Airtable. Now that's what I call being strategically aligned with search intent.

Strategic Analysis through Audience Intelligence

Going further than just intent, conduct strategic analysis to understand your audience in more depth than your competitors. So, instead of simply cranking out one content piece after another for the sake of merely having a lot of content, be more intentional and deliberate.

Do your research. Conduct audience intelligence. Talk to prospects. Interview customers. Learn from your sales and support teams.

Uncover the most popular content sources for the audience. What are their go-to websites? What are the YouTube channels they view the most? How about podcasts? What are influencers in the industry saying?

Speaking of YouTube, when was the last time you really analyzed what was going on in YouTube in your industry? I meet far too many marketers who have no idea. It's as if YouTube doesn't really exist or that their audience doesn't watch any videos (even though there are millions of views by their target audience).

Too much of the content you see online today is boring, static, and lifeless. It's content for the sake of content.

It may be based on a target keyword, but here's the thing: it also needs to resonate with the audience. With content, you're trying to speak to a real human being. Why don't more marketers act like it?

SEO and Content Marketing

To speak to a real human being, you need to know what they care about. And why.

If someone is searching in Google for green technology solutions to reduce their company's energy bills, it's not just that they care about energy bills. You need to unpack everything that they are likely thinking. What catalyzed their search? What's the backstory? What are the unspoken problems behind the scenes? How are they feeling? Why are they looking for green tech solutions specifically? What are the ramifications if they don't reduce their bills? Dig deeper, and your content will be more powerful and will consequently produce higher ROI.

Being strategic with your content means understanding your audience deeply, and then answering their questions and helping them achieve their objectives. Identify the audience-solution fit. In other words, where's the precise point where you can help them the most?

In addition, audience intelligence should include an understanding of how you'll captivate them and how you'll move them to action. That's an essential ingredient in generating ROI for your business from your content.

A Crazy Valuable Blog

When talking of content, there are a variety of formats that you can create for your audience. Regardless of the formats you choose, I would argue that a blog should be included in your content marketing mix.

There are entire industries where blogging is rare. That blows my mind. Blogging is low-hanging fruit for putting valuable content in front of your target audience throughout the customer journey. If you do it strategically, your content helps with not only Google organic rankings, but also conversions, lead generation, and ultimately more revenue.

I could write an entire book about the benefits of blogging. I'll summarize a few of the key ones for you here:

- Blogging enables you to answer your prospects' questions, connect with them on their interests, help solve their problems, and empower them to achieve objectives.
- With well researched and thoughtful blog posts, you establish your business as a thought leader.
- With so much content on the page, blogging is a great way to showcase your brand personality and differentiation.
- Blogging is an effective way to increase your organic visibility in Google.
- It drives a great deal of qualified traffic to your website.
- Blogs can act as the source for content atomization. For example, you can create a checklist, workbook, emails, and video based on the content from one blog post.
- You can take ideas from your blog posts and use them in your social media posts, helping you to get more value from your investment in each post.
- You can re-engage and reactivate past customers.
- Through strategic calls-to-action, blogging helps you convert site visitors into actual leads.

Here's the problem, though. Even with so many benefits for your business, many B2B blogs are boring and ineffective. There's very little thought put into them other than adding accurate information to a page. It's as if checking the "publish blog post" box on a to-do list were the objective instead of adding value to the reader and making them want to do business with you.

Remember, there's a real human being reading your content. Would you strive to make your next sales pitch boring? Of course not.

So, then, why would your blog be treated mostly as an afterthought? Your blog is a veritable pitch. The post may not be directly trying to push any of your products or services, but it is an important touch point with your prospective customers. With long-form content, they may be on your page for several minutes. This is a unique chance to captivate them and start building a relationship.

To that end, aim to make your blog crazy valuable. If you can make your blog something they look forward to turning to, time and time again, then you'll be using your blog as an actual business builder.

SEO Topic Clusters

There are dozens of types of content online. Among all of them, what's one of the most effective for getting your content onto Google page one?

SEO topic clusters.

Back in the early days of SEO, it was all about optimizing individual pages for specific keywords. When the Google Hummingbird algorithm update hit in 2013, though, focusing on topic areas rather than individual keywords became a smarter SEO strategy. As a result, one page could rank for dozens of related terms. Similarly, ranking for a range of terms across your content would not only help those particular pages, but your entire site. In other words, a rising tide would lift all ships.

In order to help Google understand your expertise, broader topics were helpful. And in order to help your target audience, as well, it made sense to organize content within topics.

Thus, the SEO topic cluster strategy was born.

Topic clusters are a cleaner architecture for your content. Plus, they are exceptionally effective at helping your content to rank organically in Google.

So, what exactly are topic clusters?

SEO topic clusters are a hub-and-spoke model of content building, centered on specific topic areas. A single "pillar" page acts as the hub, optimized to the main topic term you want the page to ultimately rank for. You then surround the pillar page with a variety of sub-pages, or "cluster pages", which focus on narrower topics within the overarching topic of the pillar page.

It's much like a bicycle wheel. For example, a pillar page might focus on "accounting software". Your cluster pages in that case might include:

- Best accounting software
- Online accounting software
- Easy accounting software
- Small business accounting software
- Business tax software
- Accounting software for MAC
- Accounting software for PC
- Types of accounting software
- What to look for when purchasing accounting software
- Accounting apps

- Etc.

The pillar page should link out to each of these cluster pages, and each cluster page should link back to the pillar page. In certain cases, you may want to build 15 or 20 cluster pages in support of an SEO topic cluster. In other cases, perhaps only five or six cluster pages make sense. Regardless, think of these internal links as the glue that holds your content structure together while giving Google a clear view of the relationship among the many content pieces.

You may be thinking that this sounds like the Tree Ring Multiplier Strategy explained earlier in this chapter. And you would be correct. The main difference is that with the Tree Ring Multiplier Strategy, you're restricted by your current Google page one rankings. The main goal is to capitalize on low-hanging fruit, even though the first keyword you tackle might not be the most important to your business. The idea is to establish a foothold, so that you start gaining Google's trust more quickly, with the idea that a rising tide lifts all boats.

With SEO topic clusters, the most effective usage is when you create them based on what's most important to your business. You may not be ranking on Google page one, two, three, or ten when you start building a new topic cluster. However, this content structure is most effective when you target topics that would have the greatest impact on your business. This is not necessarily low-hanging fruit, but instead a long-term, strategic investment for the future.

As mentioned above, SEO topic clusters is largely the model we relied on to increase organic blog page views by 6,112 percent for one of our clients. It works!

Internal Linking

If you want your SEO topic clusters to be effective, spend time on internal linking. This is an area of SEO that is often overlooked. Yet, it delivers a powerful punch.

This is low-hanging fruit. Add relevant internal links within your topic clusters, and you'll improve the results from those clusters.

Someone who understands internal linking better than anyone I know is Jonas Sickler, SEO Manager at the organic search company Terakeet. Here is how Sickler looks at internal linking.

"Efficiency is the biggest barrier to overcome in SEO.

"Over the last decade, the price tag of high quality, sustainable SEO programs has risen significantly for two primary reasons: First, advances in Google's search algorithm have made spammy tactics less effective and rewarded websites that provide high-quality user experiences. And second, global enterprise brands with massive budgets have entered the fray, demanding large-scale SEO packages that require a staggering amount of resources from highly-skilled teams.

"As more big brands pour money into creating amazing digital content experiences, sourcing expertly-written copy, and securing higher quality backlinks, they must find ways to amplify efficiencies. If they don't, they risk eroding the most attractive benefit of organic search: low cost customer acquisition.

"Internal links are the key."

Sickler recommends thinking of internal links like wires. "They pass both power and information from one URL to another.

These links allow you to funnel backlink value to the most important pages on your website — especially those sections that don't earn many backlinks on their own. Equally important, they pass valuable contextual information from page to page, helping Google to understand the topics and subtopics on your domain, as well as your level of expertise."

But, just like you have different types of wires in your home, Sickler points out that there are different types of internal links within your website. Some are more valuable than others, and it's critical to prioritize the most valuable kinds of links. When creating an internal linking strategy, Sickler explains that you should strive to pass maximum context from surrounding content and link equity from organically strong pages.

Navigational links in your header and footer are primarily for users. They're on almost every page of your site, so they pass very little SEO value. Similarly, sidebar and inline CTA links are considered more supplemental, promotional, or temporary, and not a permanent part of the primary content. It makes sense when you think about it. Most people don't link to content because of a sidebar or a CTA. They link to it because of the value the main content provides.

So, which internal links provide the most value?

Sickler says, "Links within the main content area, whether that's on a category page, or within the copy of a blog post, pass along the most context and PageRank."

He recommends that when you add internal links to your pages, you consider the following questions:

1. How much SEO equity does the page have to pass along to other pages?

2. Is the internal link contextually relevant?
3. Would a user click the link and find value?

Creative Content Through Surveys

Along with SEO topic clusters, surveys are effective in generating content results. However, when you look at how many companies conduct surveys, they tap only a small percentage of their potential.

I previously explained why surveys were such a useful VoC tool for your business for uncovering audience insight.

I want you to rethink surveys in terms of lead generating content, as well. Instead of just a one-time vehicle for data gathering that then is added to a report, think bigger. Before you even begin your survey, brainstorm different ways to package and promote the survey results to 10X your exposure.

Surveys are not only a lead generation tool, they are a quadruple threat. They enable you to:

1. Capture VoC
2. Create unique, authentic content from the insight derived
3. Capture media attention, online shares, and backlinks from the content. Use your creativity to focus on topics that are captivating.
4. Generate new leads

As I had mentioned in the previous chapter, for one client in the healthcare space, our team at Stratabeat wanted to tap into the authentic, real-world stories of registered nurses instead of simply writing about them. So, we conducted a national survey.

The survey for our healthcare client resulted in roughly 3,500 responses, including emotional stories and unique qualitative insight, from a wide range of nurses across the U.S. From this, we created a range of content, including a series of blog posts, a report, an infographic, and two SlideShare decks.

We were able to get full-page coverage in the largest website in the industry along with media coverage in a wide range of websites. In addition, the blog posts created in support of the survey were the most popular and most viewed for the entire year for the client. They also generated the most backlinks that year. The SlideShare reports alone generated more than 32,000 views.

All of this activity helped our client get spotted by a national TV show, which invited the CEO onto the show to be interviewed. This then led to four additional national TV appearances that year. The survey was a PR and SEO rocket ship.

One survey. Five national TV appearances. Not bad.

ANOTHER EXAMPLE of creative thinking in survey planning is a story that SEO expert, advisor, and author Eli Schwartz told me.

When Schwartz was at SurveyMonkey as their Director of Growth & SEO, he led the SEO team in transforming organic search from an afterthought to one of the largest growth drivers at the company. He's acutely aware of the power of surveys as a PR engine (and by extension, a link building engine).

While based in Singapore leading Asia-Pacific (APAC) marketing for SurveyMonkey, Schwartz partnered with an organization called the Restroom Association of Singapore and developed a survey about people's bathroom habits. (Really!)

Schwartz had noticed how crazy attached people were to their smartphones, and so thought that the survey would help them understand just how inseparable people and mobile phones had become.

What he found was shocking. And gross!

Approximately 61 percent confirmed that they used (talk, text, browse) their phones in the bathroom. (Ironically, 44 percent still thought that using a phone in the bathroom was inappropriate.)

What they found was that the most popular smartphone bathroom activities were:

- Texting (49 percent)
- Reading email (47 percent)
- Talking (35 percent)
- Making online purchases (9 percent)

FYI, the survey also revealed that 9 percent of people have dropped a phone into the toilet. Yikes!

A major benefit of the survey was that the results were so outrageous that dozens of other websites, including sites with a massive volume of visitors such as Mashable, started linking to the survey results on the SurveyMonkey website. The survey got picked up in every English media in the entire region. The campaign cost only a few hundred dollars yet netted a great deal of awareness and backlinks.

It's sometimes a challenge for any one piece of content to generate a substantial amount of backlinks. In this case, the data allowed SurveyMonkey to create multiple pieces of content, and to repeat the process by running the survey year after year, further expanding their reach and augmenting their backlink volume.

Original Research

With surveys, you conduct original research, which can then be used to create unique content. But you don't necessarily need surveys when creating research-based content. There are various additional techniques for gathering data, as well, such as mining public data, mining your own data, live interviews, etc.

Research-based content is one of the most effective strategies for hitting a content home run. And what I love about original research is that it's inherently unique and something your competitors simply cannot copy.

I spoke with Susan Moeller, who was Sr. Marketing Manager at the software company BuzzSumo at the time, and she shared that BuzzSumo's most successful posts were those based on research and analysis of large data sets. For example, titles such as: "400,000 Articles Analyzed: Here's What We Learned About Content Engagement".

Moeller explained, "The research forms the base of the blog post. The process is time intensive, but the result is unique. Content created this way drives traffic, generates brand awareness, and helps position BuzzSumo as an industry thought leader. It is also useful to our audience, as we are careful to add suggestions for how our conclusions can be applied."

In a study by BuzzSumo and Mantis Research, 55 percent of respondents confirmed that original research helped them with lead generation. Beyond leads, original research benefited brands through media mentions (63 percent), as well.[15] The media are eager for unique data and information that will captivate the audience. Online research helps them check the boxes on what they're looking for.

On top of all of this, original research tends to attract a great amount of online sharing and backlinks to your website, expanding your reach and boosting your organic search results. At the time of this writing, the BuzzSumo post mentioned above had driven more than a thousand backlinks from 500+ websites. Imagine compounding these types of results with a library of research pieces.

Another example of original research-based content is a database of B2B websites that Stratabeat has built. The database includes a number of website quality factors, such as design, UX, optimization, content, CTAs, etc. Based on an analysis of the data, we've secured speaking gigs and spoken at various industry events sharing our findings. This has enabled us to get in front of thousands of additional audience members, which of course is invaluable.

And here's yet one more example for you. Stratabeat works with one of our clients in producing a series of industry market share reports. We leverage the client's proprietary technology to organize and extract the data for analysis. Each report contains hundreds of data points, and enables our client to offer reports that no competitor can match.

The reports are offered on the client's website, along with a number of related blog posts. Collectively, they have garnered press coverage and have generated more than 35,000 page views.

A major benefit of producing research-based reports for this client is that not only do they use them on their website as lead magnets, but they also use them in targeted LinkedIn as well as ABM campaigns. In other words, they are not only great for SEO and attracting traffic and backlinks, but also for targeted outreach.

So, if you're looking to produce highly unique content that helps you cut through all the noise, consider content based on original research.

Free Tools

This tactic was covered in the Lateral Thinking And Creativity chapter earlier in the book, but it's so powerful I want to reinforce it here.

To drive more traffic, shares, backlinks, and leads, consider creating a free tool within your website that your target audience will genuinely find useful. You may be hesitant to invest the effort in building a tool, only to give it away for free. But as you've already read, the results can be off the charts. Offering a free online tool is one of the most effective ways to exponentially increase backlinks to your website, one of the most important ingredients in improving your organic search rankings.

An example I provided earlier was the Pingdom Website Speed Test. The free tool enables you to test the page load speed of any web page from various servers located around the world. By offering it for free, the company has generated more than 4.4 million backlinks from 35,000+ third-party websites. On top of this, the tool has attracted roughly 150,000 in monthly organic traffic.

Other examples of free online tools that also do the triple-duty of attracting qualified traffic, generating backlinks, and delivering new leads, include:

- Tableau Public, Tableau's free data visualization tool available to the public, has generated a great deal of usage and more than 9 million backlinks.
- CoSchedule's Headline Analyzer Tool has generated more than 25,000 backlinks.
- Bankrate has a business loan calculator with 6,500+ backlinks.
- Wonder Unit's Storyboarder tool has attracted more than 4,200 backlinks.
- Canva's Color Wheel tool has more than 3,800 backlinks.

Whether it's a few hundred backlinks or a few million, free tools can be ridiculously effective at driving leads. Look at every single one of those backlinks as being a virtual salesperson for your company, guiding folks from around the web to your site. Just remember that any tool you develop needs to offer true value to your audience.

Long-form Content

Want another content format that gets results?

If you're looking to get onto Google page one, it's hard to beat long-form content. Semrush's *The State of Content Marketing 2020 Global Report*, which analyzed more than 1.2 million blog posts, reveals that 7,000+ word posts generate 3X more page views and 43 percent more online shares than shorter posts (900-1,200 words).[16]

According to a separate Semrush Google ranking factors study, content ranking in the top three positions in Google is 45 percent longer than the content ranking in position 20 on average.[17]

These are some of the benefits of long-form content, but the benefits don't stop there.

Long-form content is great for readers, as it can provide them with a rich educational or entertainment experience. The content is long enough to allow the author or authors to go into depth into topics, and readers can extract a good deal of value in minutes.

However, it would be shortsighted to see the value of long-form content in only the words and images on the page.

Long-form content can be used as a funnel to drive more value for your business.

First, in attracting traffic, long-form content typically makes for high converting landing pages. The experience on the page can be more fulfilling. Plus, the pages answer so many of the questions in the mind of the site visitor that CTAs tend to work well in driving them to action. By incorporating links or offers for contextually relevant, value-added content (e.g., whitepaper, research report, webinar, course, demo, etc.), you can tie promotions directly to landing pages.

And once you have them reading the content, there are various ways to capitalize on the traffic in delivering a richer experience aligned with your business interests. In any website, there are typically "money pages" that drive leads or revenue. For example, product pages, services pages, request-a-demo pages, webinar landing pages, etc. Long-form content performs well in our experience in funneling your site visitors to the areas of your site that matter most to your business. In your content, include calls-to-action (CTAs) that guide your readers to the next step. The key is that it really and truly needs to deliver added value to the site visitor.

Let's take a Stratabeat blog post as an example. In a long-form post about high performance B2B websites (more than 4,200 words), for instance, we include multiple inline CTAs inviting the individual to contact us to explore transforming their B2B website into a high performance growth engine for their business. The page already provides the reader with many recommendations for their B2B website, and the CTAs help them take the next step towards execution. Those CTAs have brought us not only new leads, but also new clients.

So when crafting long-form content, don't just limit your brand to a certain number of words per page. Think of your content as a funnel. Based on the content on the page, what are contextually relevant next steps for them to take that (1) provide them with additional value, (2) help them achieve their goal or objective, and (3) benefit your business?

A perk of long-form content that is not commonly written about is that it can be an excellent petri dish for testing and experimentation. Because there's so much real estate on the page, there's ample opportunity to test a number of different hypotheses.

For example, experiment with different content lengths to see what performs best in Google organic search. Test the inclusion of different content elements, whether charts, surveys, tools, or types of visuals, to see what generates the most online shares. Test a new page layout and see if that impacts organic search or online sharing, or both. Test CTAs to see what converts at the highest rate.

Test as much as you can to extract as much value out of the content as possible.

Shareable Content

One problem that I see all the time with B2B content is that... it's just not that interesting. It may focus on a particular topic, it may be accurate, and it may be useful, but too often the authoring team forgets that an actual human being is going to read it.

We're talking snoozeville!

My recommendation is to try to make your content *captivating*. Make it elicit an emotional response. Make it spark the imagination. Make it increase curiosity. Make it stop them in their tracks. Make it force them to think.

In his book *Contagious: Why Things Catch On*, Jonah Berger explores the psychology of social transmission. Specifically, he looks at what makes something go viral. He found that content that evokes an emotional response is more likely to be shared with others. And digging even deeper, he found that emotional arousal drives sharing, meaning that evoking stronger emotions tends to increase sharing even more.

In many years of managing content projects for clients, and even in watching the results of Stratabeat's own content, I have found a few additional factors that help to drive sharing.

For example, content that's based on original research (see my comments on this above) tends to drive a great deal of sharing, as long as it's promoted well. This is one of the most effective ways to achieve virality in B2B.

Another method is the use of powerful statistics. The more that a surprising or impressive stat is highlighted towards the beginning of a content piece, the more likely it is to be shared.

When explaining a concept, give an example. Instead of *telling* them, *show* them. We are visual creatures. Roughly half of the neurons in our brains are dedicated to vision. Humans enjoy the experience more when information is easy to ingest, process, and understand. Making it visual with an actual example of what you're talking about achieves this in spades.

Yet one more way to increase content sharing is to wrap your information in stories. When a person reads a story, their brain chemistry actually changes. The brain releases oxytocin and reduces cortisol and pain. The physiological and psychological effects of storytelling are undeniable. According to cognitive psychologist Jerome Bruner, a fact wrapped in a story is 22X more memorable than the mere presentation of that information.

But how many times do you read a content piece that doesn't include any of these elements? Often, right?

If you want better content results, rethink your content. Evoke a high-arousal response, make use of original research, highlight surprising statistics, include actual examples, and employ more storytelling. And then watch the volume of online shares of your content increase.

Answering Questions

When marketing teams plan their content calendar, it's often from the viewpoint of topics of interest among their target audience. That's a good start, but it's only half of the story.

The other half is the specific questions they are asking. The way that people often think is through questions. When they are not actively talking, they are asking and answering questions inside their minds throughout the day. Developing a content strategy based on questions is a highly effective way of ensuring your content resonates with your audience.

Let's say your team thinks of a number of content pieces you'd like to publish about business plans. Take the topics a step further by thinking through all the questions your audience is asking at the beginning, the middle, and the end of their journey.

For example, "how to write a business plan", "how to write an executive summary for a business plan", "how to do market research for a business plan", "how to write a business plan for potential investors", "what are the most common mistakes made when creating a business plan", or "what are examples of successful business plans", etc.

Questions are the basis of a vast number of online searches, in which individuals are looking for guidance, solutions, and answers. The more you can understand the questions they're asking, the greater your ability to provide them with information that they'll find highly relevant and useful.

But how can you uncover the questions that they are asking?

As mentioned earlier, start with voice of the customer (VoC) by interviewing customers and learning from your salespeople and support team. Beyond that, there's a treasure trove of questions being asked online.

You can start with Google itself. Many keyword research tools identify these questions. Some are baked into a larger suite of tools, but also you can search in Google for dedicated question-answering tools that reveal the questions being asked online.

In addition, look in the Google search engine results pages (SERPs) themselves. There, you'll often find what's called People

Also Ask (PAA) boxes, which answer questions related to a given search query.

Another relevant Google SERP feature is the "Related Searches" found in the Google search results. Even if many of the related searches are not questions, often a few questions are included.

The Google Question Hub features questions asked in Google that have yet to be answered online. This is a unique opportunity to get out ahead of the competition in providing your audience with answers they are already seeking but not finding.

You should go beyond Google, as well. Questions are also being asked in other search engines such as Bing, Yahoo, and DuckDuckGo. You'll find questions being asked in YouTube and Twitter, and on Q&A sites like Quora and forums. Search around for FAQs online, too.

Questions are everywhere!

When I talked with Masha Finkelstein when she was Director of Demand Generation at Betterworks — she has since had roles in Growth Marketing at Google and Marketing Technology Innovation at Intuit — she explained that Quora was a surprising success for the performance management solutions company.

"Quora has proven very effective for us in driving high converting website traffic," Finkelstein told me. "It's a free resource, which makes it extra special. Answering questions with timely and relevant information that people are looking for as related to your products — what can be better?"

Finkelstein is correct. What could be better than answering your prospective customers' questions at the precise time that they are seeking answers? It's a unique brand touch point, and given the personalized nature of the engagement can easily lead to the generation of new leads.

Creating content based on the questions they are asking is a surprisingly effective way to reach highly targeted and highly qualified prospects, even if search volume is low. And that's a critical point. If you know the specific questions they need answered at the bottom of the funnel in order to cross the finish line in purchasing your products or services, then you'd be crazy not to proactively address them with your content, regardless of the search volume.

Going Hollywood

When talking about content marketing, the conversation often revolves around text-based forms of content. For example, blog posts, articles, guides, whitepapers, ebooks, reports, case studies, and presentations.

However, be careful not to forget about the power of video.

YouTube is the second most popular search engine (after Google, of course), with more than two billion people currently accessing it monthly.

And video means business when it comes to lead generation. Aberdeen Group reports that companies using video in their marketing generate a 66 percent higher website conversion rate than those who don't use video.[18] Wyzowl research uncovered that 84 percent of video marketers believe that video has helped them generate leads, while 78 percent report that video has directly helped increase sales.[19]

Video is one of the most engaging and captivating forms of B2B marketing. Too many B2B marketers ignore video in their marketing, but video helps boost your lead generation results and so should be seriously considered.

The options for using video are seemingly endless. You can embed a video in a blog, summarizing the main points or alternatively digging deeper into one aspect of the post. You can share a demo or even specific product features. You can create a how-to video. You can share informal, quick-hitting, point-of-view (POV) videos on LinkedIn. Interviewing industry leaders is another option, as is showcasing customer stories or capturing customer testimonials. Or you can create something simply meant to entertain your audience. Some companies have been known to even create documentaries. The sky's the limit.

As I often say, for greater impact, strive to evoke an emotional response from your audience. There's a lot of B2B video content that simply attempts to communicate information accurately, without regard for generating an emotional reaction from viewers. Video is a unique medium that better enables you to connect with them on a deeper level. You'll have more success if you engage with your audience on a subconscious level by connecting with them emotionally.

With emotional impact in mind, it's useful (though highly counterintuitive) to understand that sometimes culture-focused content (when done right) performs even better as a lead driver than demand generation campaigns.

Tyer Lessard, VP Marketing and Chief Video Strategist at Vidyard, a video platform company, shared surprising lead generation results with me from the company's culture-oriented videos. Lessard pointed out that this type of content has not only helped to build brand and create a more personal connection with prospective customers, but has also effectively translated into leads and pipeline. Even something like a holiday video campaign, in which the aim was simply to thank customers and prospects for being part of the Vidyard community and "to put a smile on their faces", generated amazing results. In other words, the company was not even trying to generate leads, yet this video emerged as the top performing campaign for an entire year in terms of pipeline and revenue attribution. The friendliness of the campaign apparently opened up the audience to having many more conversations.

Why have culture videos worked so well for Vidyard? I think it's because at the end of the day, your audience is made up of real human beings. With feelings. With emotions. Your audience doesn't scroll through their options in Netflix in order to find boring movies or shows. Instead, they are looking for something that will move them. Similarly, your lead generation efforts through video should aim to move them.

Another counter-intuitive approach that Lessard and team implemented was to make the sales team an inclusive part of a major content campaign workflow (as opposed to simply handing off leads to them at the end of the process). One example of this was through the development of an interactive assessment tool. Instead of spitting out automated results or an automated email, the results were delivered one-to-one by an actual salesperson. Prior to delivering the results, the salesperson would spend time learning about their business and website so as to have higher-quality conversations with audience members who had taken the assessment. Lessard confirmed that this has been highly successful in generating pipeline for Vidyard, proving that sometimes you just need to rethink your approach to video marketing in order to achieve higher ROI.

Increasing Your Video ROI

Want easy ways (that your competition is most likely ignoring) to increase the ROI of your video efforts even further?

First, focus on the content in your videos. Vidyard's Lessard, in one of the instructional videos on the Vidyard website, points out the power of simply creating videos that follow a "They Ask, You Answer" format. In other words, what are the specific questions that your audience is asking in the initial and mid-stages of the customer journey. Then, create short, focused videos answering these questions very directly. Each video would answer one targeted question. In this way, your video marketing would be perfectly aligned with what your audience is looking for.

Another approach is to use video to increase the ROI of other lead generation initiatives in a supportive role. For example, a video trailer could be created to heighten awareness and interest in an upcoming whitepaper, research report, webinar, or event. If you think of it as something similar to a movie trailer, you can see how it could get your audience excited for upcoming content offerings, boosting your campaigns' ultimate performance.

You can also include CTAs in your videos in order to increase ROI. This can take the form of a pre-roll gate, requiring input of an email address or other information in order to unlock the video. Or, the CTA may take the form of a mid-roll annotation. Alternatively, it could be an end card in your video. But it could also be as simple as the person featured in a video asking the audience to take a specific action. You can also include CTAs in your video description on YouTube.

Include multiple CTAs. Include them everywhere!

If you're not yet posting video content to LinkedIn, start today. In our experience across a range of B2B clients in various industries, video just about always outperforms other types of content in LinkedIn. For a new biotech startup, our videos generated more than 25,000 video views inside of LinkedIn alone within two and a half months.

Video + LinkedIn = ROI.

Yet another ROI-generating activity is how you structure the video production itself. Think like the TV show Shark Tank. When they prepare for a new season, they shoot all episodes at once, over a few days. In this way, you can shoot an entire series of short videos in a day.

Or, you can shoot a longer video, and then slice and dice the content into snackable videos for your website, blog, and social media. Whenever you can shoot once and reuse multiple times, you should do it.

Want even greater ROI from your video investment?

You can also use data to increase your video ROI. Once you've collected enough data to determine which videos are clear winners for your business, turn the top performers into a series. You've already done the hard job of creating videos. Now, consistently produce similar videos that keep adding value. The result should be a compound effect. Someone who likes your series is far more likely to remain engaged with your brand than someone who watches one video.

Acquiring Publications/Websites

I've written a lot in this chapter about ways to create optimized content that will help you drive greater organic traffic and leads.

When thinking about SEO and content marketing, though, there's one strategy that doesn't focus on *creation* but instead on *acquisitions*. Namely, purchasing publications that already rank high for your target keywords.

Arrow Electronics, the world's largest distributor of electronic components, is a good example of a company that went out and bought a range of publications and websites, vastly expanding its content footprint. In the process, it *became the media* for its audience of electronics engineers.

In 2015, Arrow acquired United Technical Publishing, a digital provider of product information to the electronics components industry, from Hearst Corporation. United Technical Publishing's portfolio at the time included directories, newsletters, engineering-driven websites, tools, and databases.[20]

In 2016, Arrow acquired UBM's technology and electronic design-related global internet media portfolio. The publications and websites included EE Times, EDN, ESM, Embedded, EBN, TechONline, and Datasheets.com.[21]

In total, Arrow purchased more than 50 media properties in those two years. Not only did they gain control of the content from the acquisitions, they also gained access to the editorial talent in order to continue the flow of content. In the process, Arrow established itself as the largest media company in the electronics industry.

If there are publications already performing strongly in Google on queries that you highly value, an acquisition is one of the fastest ways for you to gain an asset to help you dominate the page in Google. Not only that, but like Arrow Electronics, you may be able to turn your content into a profit center to boot.

The Power of Creativity and Imagination in Content Creation

Along with all the content that you can create (or acquire) to drive massive volumes of organic traffic, I want to urge you at the same time to think creatively. Sometimes, the value that you derive from your content is not necessarily search visibility and traffic. Instead, it's about captivating your audience and building a relationship.

You can do this effectively through extreme creativity. Take an idea, and just run with it as far as you can go.

A good example of this is Wistia's "Video Marketing Week" campaign a few years ago. Barb Gagne, Director of Demand Gen at the video hosting company Wistia at the time of the campaign and now Director of Digital Marketing at the security software company Cybereason, walked me through the campaign from an insider's perspective.

"Video Marketing Week" was not an actual thing at the time. Wistia invented it!

Barb shared her excitement at just how successful the event turned out to be. "It surprised me that a brand could literally invent an event like Video Marketing Week, and promote it to their loyal audiences, and attract new audiences in such an effective way."

The purpose was to educate marketers and provide them with a week's worth of content all about doing better marketing with video. It was promoted as an "online crash course in all things video marketing". The event was filled with live sessions and webinars with Wistia's marketing team, as well as downloadable guides, templates, worksheets, and tools. Each day of the week focused on an individual component of video marketing, from setting the strategy to promoting videos to optimizing videos to reporting on performance. The goal was to give marketers the know-how to get started with video marketing.

Wistia promoted Video Marketing Week for three weeks leading up to the event. They brainstormed and used a combination of owned and paid social media, emails to the Wistia database, website promotions, and influencer marketing. In addition, employees created promo videos and posted them on LinkedIn on the same day/time as a takeover, leading to 25,000+ video views on LinkedIn alone.

The results of the promotional efforts far exceeded the Wistia team's expectations. At the end of the three-week promotional phase, they had generated 9,500 leads. Enhancing the ROI of the effort, they configured the event page post-event to be a consolidated hub for all of the campaign content, enabling the content to act as a lead generator on an ongoing basis.

So, remember, not all content needs to be geared for SEO. Sometimes, you just want to excite and captivate them!

Bottom-Of-The-Funnel Content

If you look around the web for content development and content marketing advice, you'll find a great deal of the focus is on top-of-the-funnel content. This is for people who just identified a pain point or problem to be solved, or alternatively a goal to be achieved. They are starting to explore. Yes, content that serves those just starting their journey is extremely important.

However, I urge you to also create content for the bottom of the funnel. These are people who have done their research and compared options. They are on the cusp of making a purchase decision. Bottom-of-the-funnel content can supercharge the ROI of your content. And it's an area of content development where many B2B businesses overlook the opportunity.

This can mean the creation of content that helps a prospective customer make the final decision to purchase from you. That would include case studies, direct comparisons, competitive matrices, ROI calculators, TCO (total cost of ownership) calculators and other tools, etc. These are invaluable in helping them to make a decision.

A stack of case studies may have zero search volume, but that's irrelevant. What's critical is moving them towards a final purchase decision, and case studies are an effective way to move them in that direction.

Building a bottom-of-the-funnel content moat may also mean getting very specific with your content.

For example, if your audience is looking to find web design services, a post at the top of the funnel may be focused on web design principles. But then as they are about to make a final decision, offer content that is more narrowly focused, such as how to increase the ROI of a green technology company website, how to increase the conversion rates of a software website, common mistakes to avoid when developing a biotech website, or a comparison of your souped-up WordPress website development process vs. the industry standard. Each of these will appeal to a smaller, more targeted audience, but that's the entire point. It might be a smaller audience, but it will be harder hitting as it will speak to their specific interests.

General, broad strokes don't work at the bottom of the funnel. Precision, specificity, and customization do.

Google E-A-T

No matter if your content is at the bottom, middle, or top of the funnel, figure out how to incorporate or factor Google E-A-T into your web pages. E-A-T stands for expertise, authoritativeness, and trustworthiness.

I talk with many marketers, and even today, many of them have never heard of Google E-A-T. That needs to change. If you are involved in SEO and content, an understanding of E-A-T is essential for your future Google organic search success.

Google E-A-T comes from Google's Search Quality Rater Guidelines, which is an official Google document referenced by human quality raters who are tasked with assessing the quality of Google search results.

The bottom line? You need to clarify your credentials for writing the content you're putting out into the world. It needs to be clear to the human quality raters. If your content is related to health technology, for example, then you may need a physician writing the content or at least reviewing it, and that should be clear on the page. You may want to display logos of any medical associations that your organization belongs to. You may want to include testimonials from physicians. You may want to highlight any health tech patents you have been granted. You get the idea.

Google E-A-T is especially important for topics related to health, wealth, and well-being. These are what Google refers to as YMYL (Your Money or Your Life) topics.

This may be news to you, but if you produce content in these areas, it's absolutely critical that you start layering in more and more proof of your credibility now, so that Google doesn't start disqualifying your content.

Using AI for Higher Rankings

If you've written a piece of content, you might think that you're ready to publish it. However, that would be skipping an all-important part of today's SEO — the incorporation of artificial intelligence (AI) into your research, content creation, workflow, content grading, and quality assurance.

In recent years, AI-based SEO tools such as Clearscope, MarketMuse, and Surfer have entered the market, and to me, they are a game changer. Essentially, what these tools do is accelerate and enhance the content research and optimization process, at scale. They can look at the Google search landscape and take a data-based approach to guiding you to create the type of content that's necessary to get onto Google page one. They accomplish this through search engine results page (SERP) analysis, competitive intelligence, and relational analysis.

What some of them can do is guide you through the research process and even help you with building your customer journey and content briefs. They then advise you on your headings and body copy as well as related keywords to include on the page.

I would advise against relying on AI for actual copy production itself at the current time. Our agency has tested a handful of tools, and none of them produced copy as clearly, cohesively, and effectively as an actual person. With that being said, AI-powered SEO tools are exceptionally helpful in the areas of research, customer journeys, and content briefs.

Beyond research, customer journeys, and content briefs, AI-based tools aid you in the copywriting and copyediting process. You can create and edit your content piece right within the application itself, either from scratch or once you have a draft of your content in hand, with real-time SEO grading. The higher your grade, the more likely it is that your content will make it onto Google page one.

I would estimate that the majority of marketing teams are not yet using AI-powered tools in their SEO and content development processes. I believe, though, that omission is going to make them less competitive. It's an opportunity for you to leapfrog them. Our agency has seen tremendous results through the use of these types of tools. We are true believers. If you recall the blogging example I had mentioned earlier where Stratabeat helped a client to increase organic page views sourced by the search engines by 6,112 percent, one of the ingredients in achieving such massive traffic gains was our use of AI-based optimization technology.

Dominating the Page

OK, let's say you've followed the recommendations in this chapter and you're firing on all cylinders with your optimized content development. If you're looking for a way to get even higher ROI, let's reimagine what's possible in Google. Instead of just winning, let's aim to double our winnings.

How?

Through a strategy called "Dominating the Page".

What this means is that you try to occupy as much of the screen real estate as possible on Google page one for your target keywords. With many searches, Google will limit the times your website appears organically on the search results page. With each incremental piece of real estate you capture beyond that, you're making it more likely the searcher engages with your brand. Plus, you're concurrently pushing something off of the page, oftentimes a competitor. A double win!

Another approach is to create complementary content. For example, a blog post AND a playbook. Or a web page AND an article. Or a research report AND a complementary presentation, webinar, and series of blog posts. If the search results for a target keyword include video among the Google page one results, shoot a video and optimize it to the target keyword. And if images are included in the page one results, you can similarly optimize some images for your target keyword. All of these give you an opportunity to capture incremental space on Google page one.

By targeting similar keywords with different content formats, you increase the probability of landing on page one. Plus, with so much coverage of the page, you increase the likelihood of a clickthrough.

How else can you dominate the page? Well, you can launch a targeted microsite. This would give you the opportunity to rank several more times on the page.

Or, if there's a blog in your industry that ranks exceptionally well in Google, then consider purchasing it. Remember, Arrow Electronics purchased more than 50 media properties on their path to building a veritable content empire. This is an underutilized strategy to capture more content market share.

And don't forget about all the temporal ways to occupy real estate on Google page one, when applicable. This would include press releases and Twitter posts.

Finally, you can also easily increase your real estate on the page by engaging in Google Ads.

One of our clients recently captured 50 percent of Google page one organically for their most valuable keyword. This involved the use of three separate websites and a press mention that was picked up by a news website. (They also had a paid search ad on the page.) They knocked two competitors off of the page in the process.

Think about what this does in terms of brand perception. They are being seen as the market leader. There's the added benefit of more traffic. And finally, all of this will lead to more leads and revenue, and less for the competition. We're talking about the difference in millions of dollars annually for this client.

Pruning Old Content

So far, we've been going through ways to expand your content. However, like the Ahrefs example above, you can also prune your content to massively improve marketing performance. What you want to do is eliminate any non-performing content.

Conduct an audit of your content. Categorize it by audience segment and topical category.

Then, identify any content that is not performing. If it's getting very few page views, shares, and links, consider removing it entirely and applying a 301 Redirect to the most relevant page so that any SEO equity would be passed along to a page with greater traction.

If the topic is still relevant and it's just a case of poor content, consider maintaining the URL but re-writing, upgrading, and overhauling the piece itself. This will give you a chance to resuscitate the content and breathe new life into it. In a sense, you should treat it as if you're writing the piece from scratch, with an eye towards delivering the most value to the reader of any options online. (Don't worry what was in the original. Just throw the old copy in the trash can if necessary.)

Or, perhaps you have multiple pages with similar content. There might be a good deal of overlap, for example, confusing Google as to which content piece is relevant to a query. Consider merging the pages into the strongest URL, and applying a 301 Redirect from the URLs to be eliminated. When you do that, spend the time to enhance the page with value from all sources so that what you wind up with is a supercharged version of the original content. More than just merging the pages, you want to achieve 1 + 1 = 3.

Mike Michalowicz points out in his book *The Pumpkin Plan* that farmers who grow giant, record-setting pumpkins are continually pruning away weaker pumpkins from the vine so that all the nutrients flow to the pumpkins with the greatest potential. At the end of the process, only a single pumpkin remains, receiving all the nutrients with accelerated growth. When you see photos of giant pumpkins from festivals and state fairs weighing in excess of 1,000 pounds (and sometimes over 2,000), that's the end result you are seeing.

In the same way, you want to prune your content so that you're redirecting nutrients to stronger, higher-performing pages, creating super powered content in the process. This also makes it easier for Google to understand the topics in which you're an expert and to direct traffic to the high performers. This in turn lifts the results for your content overall.

Jonas Sickler of Terakeet, introduced to you earlier in this chapter, spent eight months pruning content of an old website he was working on. In doing so, organic traffic grew from 8,598 to 30,927 – a 3.6X increase. He achieved this while adding only five new posts during that time. That's the power of content pruning!

So, although it sounds counterintuitive, before expanding your content you may want to prune it and get it into better shape first.

Repurposing Content The Right Way

To get greater ROI out of your content, repurpose and atomize it. This book kicks off with the example of how Ginger Shimp and her team at SAP took a base piece of content and then created 650 different pieces of content from it, generating a pipeline of $23 million from merely a single campaign.

That's what we're talking about when referring to repurposing your content. It's not just about taking a post and creating another derivative piece out of it. It's about thinking bigger. It's about connecting with different audience segments, engaging with your audience in different ways, and creating more business possibilities.

There are so many ways to repurpose content, it behooves any marketing team to make content repurposing an important part of the content marketing process. For example:

- Blog posts can be turned into guides or videos
- Original research can be turned into reports, presentations, infographics and other data visualizations, blog posts, and all sorts of PR materials
- A playbook can be broken down into multiple, more targeted blog posts
- Webinars can be converted into videos
- Statistics can be included in blog posts, guides, presentations, and social media posts
- Interviews with thought leaders or subject matter experts can be sliced and diced into a flow of content in

different formats, some focused on a single interview and some compiled from multiple interviews

But here's where I want you to rethink how you typically go about repurposing content. Many marketers simply move content from one format into another. For example, a podcast transcript becomes a blog post. Or, a webinar becomes a video recording.

Makes sense, but it's inherently flawed in that it's fully focused on file formats and not the audience. Take the example of the video recording of a webinar. If your prospect is interested in the topic, it doesn't mean they want to see your webinar per se. They want the most pertinent information from the webinar. That's it. Nothing else.

Instead of simply converting your content from one format to another, do this. Consider what the audience is expecting when they encounter a piece of content in a given environment and customize it accordingly each time. You essentially want to optimize the content to make it more easily consumable.

So, let's say you conduct a webinar. Instead of just offering the full recording (which is probably going to include filler content and be challenging to navigate to find useful information), break it down into a series of targeted, snackable lessons. Place these inside a page with a text introduction listing the key topic covered. In this way, the reader can easily jump to the specific content they care most about, and they can completely skip over anything that's not of interest. You could even record a quick executive summary video that directly points out the main topics and key takeaways, and include this at the top of the page. On top of all of this, you can take very brief excerpts from the webinar and post them to LinkedIn with highly specific messaging that matches the excerpt, creating a series out of the longer webinar content.

Or, if the webinar is long and includes many topics of substance with rich details included for each, break up the content into a series of blog posts, each with a video recording from the relevant segments only.

Or, take the targeted, brief video, and combine it with all other content that you have related to the topic and create a topic hub where your audience can access all of your topic-based content (not just the relevant bits from the single webinar) all in one easy-to-navigate location.

Or, you may want to create a course out of several related webinars. If you do so, you'd probably want to break down your webinar videos into 10-minute and 15-minute learning modules.

The point is, content in one format does not necessarily make it user-friendly in another format. Think of how the content could be most easily communicated to the audience, and then accommodate the changes that are needed to increase the value to the reader/viewer.

Then, include a relevant next step for them. When they consume a full webinar, perhaps the CTA is to contact your company if they are interested in learning more or in purchasing from you. But in the case that it's a targeted outtake from the webinar, perhaps a better CTA would be a related piece of content. If we're talking about a knowledge hub, you may be asking them to sign up for your mailing list. Keep the momentum going, but do so in a way that will be intuitive to your audience.

Content Distribution

Many marketing teams spend significant amounts of money and resources creating content.

Yet, I'm continually surprised at the number of companies we meet who make no attempt to amplify that content. If no one sees your content, it's likely a wasted investment. I'm sorry, but no matter how great your content may be, if you're not distributing and promoting it, you're probably going to generate only limited results from it.

Some companies who actually do content distribution limit their activities to posting links on social media. That's a start, but it's a weak effort to get your content into the hands of those who really need to see it.

For example, let's say that you want to target the C-suite of your target companies. Well, many in the C-suite do not spend their time on social media and so the vast majority of your posts may be completely ineffective at making an impact. Or if you post only a single link to each content piece in each of your social channels, the likelihood of the right person finding your content is minimal.

Instead, content distribution should be a key component of your content marketing strategy. Aside from social media, you can distribute your content in a number of different ways, including:

- PR and media outreach
- Blogger outreach
- Collaborating with influencers
- Sharing with partners
- Email marketing
- Your website and landing pages

- Your knowledge hub or blog
- Amplification by executives
- Amplification by employees
- Email signatures
- ABM campaigns
- Retargeting campaigns

To maximize your content ROI, you want to customize your outreach based on the type of content you're interested in promoting. Let's compare a blog post to a book.

With a blog post, you can promote it in relevant spots in your website, including related blog posts. You can also promote it via social media, email, and amplification by employees.

If you're trying to promote a book, you can launch a dedicated microsite. In addition, you can promote it in your website, in a custom landing page, and in a series of blog posts. One post may announce that the book is coming, another may celebrate on publication day, while others may feature excerpts or summaries of key points. And similar to a blog post, you can use social media, email marketing, and amplification by executives/employees. Video marketing would also be a good idea for a book launch. ABM? Yes, if the topic aligns with the list, then the book should absolutely be offered to your ABM contacts, as well.

With a book, you should also be promoting it through third-party properties. To that end, you can collaborate with partners and influencers on creative distribution campaigns. You should talk with bloggers to explore byline posts or interviews. And speaking of interviews, you should try to get interviewed by as many relevant blogs, podcasts, websites, magazines, radio shows, and TV shows as possible. Another effective way to distribute your book is to go where people purchase books by running ads via Amazon Ads.

So, you can see, depending on the content piece, the content distribution tactics may differ substantially.

First, make sure you're dedicating sufficient resources and time to content distribution. Second, customize your approach based on the type of content. Do these two things, and watch your content performance improve significantly.

Securing Backlinks

A backlink is a link from another website to your own. Backlinks from high-quality websites are especially important when it comes to SEO, as they send a signal to Google that your website is useful, respected, and authoritative.

You hear search marketers talking about backlinks a great deal. That's because they are one of the most important Google ranking factors. The more high-quality backlinks you have, the more likely you are to climb the Google search results.

But what's not discussed enough is that not all links are created equal...

Backlinks from high-authority websites, like major national media sites, matter more than those from lower-quality sites. Links from .edu websites carry a great deal of weight.

Once you have a link from a given website, incremental links from the same website are not going to add the same level of value. With this in mind, the number of high-quality websites pointing links at your web property is a more accurate reflection of your link equity than the volume of backlinks itself.

And links from spammy websites are not only of no value, but they could potentially start hurting your SEO equity in the case that Google interprets that the sites are associated with your brand (even if it's not true).

If a website applies a "nofollow" attribute to a link, that unfortunately means that there's little value in the link, as the signal to Google is to not follow it back to your site. It doesn't mean that there's no value, but certainly less than a link without the attribute.

And guess what? Google has broadened its definition of what a link is! Even a mere mention (without a link) is valuable. Based on US Patent 8,682,892, invented by Navneet Panda and Vladimir Ofitserov, Google has made it so traffic to your site is now in part reliant on "implied links" — i.e., plain text mentions of your brand name. That's right, mere mentions of your name now (even without a link) have bearing on your Google search ranking.

The patent identifies incoming links as "express links, implied links, or both," and further clarifies that they can be actual hyperlinks or plain text. So all incoming links — express and implied — are counted toward measuring the quality of your page.

People link to content that is highly useful, newsworthy, surprising, emotion-evoking, or entertaining. My recommendation is to focus on creating unbelievably valuable content for your audience, and the backlinks will come naturally.

Strategic Methods for Securing More Backlinks

Beyond publishing awesome content (that in and of itself should drive relevant linking), there are a few things you can do to strategically attract more high-quality backlinks.

We discussed surveys and original research and tools above. These are all-stars when it comes to link generation.

You can also do the following activities, all of which facilitate additional link building:

- Conduct attention-grabbing PR
- Publish timely content based on newsworthy topics of the day ("newsjacking")
- Become a source for journalists or bloggers
- Get sites to add a link to unlinked brand mentions
- Secure byline articles in third-party sites
- Secure interviews in third-party sites
- Use intriguing statistics
- Add video to the page
- Incorporate interactivity in the page
- Create infographics. Add a code snippet on the page for use by others that includes a link back to your page.
- Construct interesting data visualizations
- Identify the sites linking to your competitors' sites, ensure your corresponding content is far better, and conduct outreach to see if they'll link to your content
- Identify sites with relevant lists of posts or resources. Spot dead links within the lists, and pitch your own content instead.
- Look at the most popular pages in your site, and further enhance each page's appeal. Then, amplify the updated content.

- Reclaim dead backlinks on third-party websites
- Collaborate with influencers and bloggers
- Etc.

Always Be Thinking of the Future

Google evolves over time, meaning that you should keep an eye on its evolution. You don't necessarily need to be watching every single update to the search engine results pages (SERPs). However, understanding the future direction of Google is important to keep your content highly visible online.

For example, at the time of this writing, Google is working on rolling out a new technology called Multitask Unified Model (MUM). Essentially, what may take two or three or more searches today in uncovering relevant information you're seeking about a question or topic, MUM can answer in one go. It has the potential to transform how Google helps you in tackling complex tasks. MUM is even multimodal, meaning that it understands both text and images, and will likely understand video and audio in the future, too.

This is merely one example. What's important is that you keep your finger on the pulse of the future direction of the search giant, as you'll then be able to adjust your SEO and content strategies in a timely manner, ahead of the curve.

Treating Your Content As A Portfolio

If you really want to rethink your content for greater ROI, start treating your content as a portfolio just as you would a financial investment portfolio. What this means is identifying your different types of content, your various content objectives, and modeling a portfolio that delivers ample diversification to maximize the benefit to your business. You want your content to strengthen your business overall, as that will only help to accelerate leads and revenue growth. After all, just as a diversified investment portfolio tends to yield the highest returns over time, a diversified content portfolio delivers meaningful impact to your business in multiple ways.

For example, your portfolio may include the following types of content:

- **Optimized Content:** Optimized web pages, blog posts, articles, videos, etc. for greater visibility and reach in Google.
- **Link Magnets:** Content likely to attract a high volume of inbound links.
- **Gated Content:** Whitepapers, ebooks, webinars, research reports, or other content pieces for which you require the site visitor's email address for access.
- **PR Pieces:** Initiatives that help you to gain media attention and expand your reach.
- **Thought Leadership:** Content that positions your brand as a leader in the industry.
- **Opinion Pieces:** When you take a stand and share your point of view.
- **Promotional Content:** Items that directly promote your products, services, or other aspects of your brand.
- **Corporate Culture Pieces:** Content such as "Day in the Life", "Behind the Scenes", and "Community Involvement" pieces focused on promoting your internal culture.
- **Sales Enablement Content:** Materials such as case studies that help your sales team to make more sales.

By approaching your content as a portfolio, you'll have better control of your content planning and calendar, which also helps you to ensure the quality of your content. In addition, you'll be able to achieve strong results in different areas of your business, whether Google organic rankings or new qualified leads or sales team support.

Chapter Summary

SEO and content marketing are a powerful combination. SEO helps your brand to gain visibility, expand reach, and drive traffic growth. Content marketing, in turn, helps you to convert your audience into new, qualified leads for your business.

The combination of SEO and content translates into an effective lead generation flywheel. The results compound over time, making it a ridiculously effective business builder.

However, many companies are treading water when it comes to SEO and content, pouring resources into them year after year without any results. Follow the recommendations listed throughout this chapter to turn things around and to start generating a steady flow of new leads.

- When you create content for your brand, be sure to make amazing content that your target audience will be thrilled to read (or at the very least will find extremely useful).
- Target topics where you are already strong, and focus, augment, and amplify your efforts from there. In other words, if you already are ranking on Google page one for a keyword or a few keywords, target related, adjacent long-tail keywords.

- Another area to focus on early in your SEO initiatives is Google page two and page three. Do what it takes to get these keywords onto Google page one. This is low hanging fruit.
- B2B sales often involve multiple people on the buyer side. Plan and build content for the different members of the decision-making team.
- Similarly, develop different content pieces for the multiple steps in the buyer journey. It's critical that you're supplying them with the right information at each stage of the journey.
- When creating content optimized to a keyword, aligning with search intent for that keyword is critically important.
- Go beyond search data to understand your audience. Layer in audience intelligence from surveys, interviews, YouTube, podcasts, etc.
- In your marketing mix, include a blog, which delivers countless benefits to your business.
- When organizing content around your most important topics, construct SEO topic clusters for better Google rankings. Implement internal links among the pillar page and various cluster pages within each topic cluster so that it's clearer for Google to understand the relationship among the pages.
- Content based on original research is one of the most powerful forms of B2B content.
- Developing a free tool is one of the most effective ways to generate links from third-party websites.
- There are many benefits of long-form content, including better organic search performance as well as the ability to dive deep into topics, showcase your

- expertise, differentiate your brand, and include multiple CTAs to drive them to a next step.
- Your audience is likely asking many questions online. As such, it's a good strategy to strive to answer those questions in your website and content.
- Video is an effective medium for captivating and engaging your audience. Develop a video strategy and incorporate specific CTAs both inside and outside the videos themselves.
- Complementary to creating content, consider acquiring publications/websites that are already ranking on Google page one for a set of your target keywords. This is how Arrow Electronics became the largest media player in the electronics industry.
- Creativity is often underappreciated in business, but by applying creativity and imagination to your content creation you'll be better able to captivate your audience and achieve greater marketing ROI as a result.
- Content marketers often focus on broad, head terms at the top of the funnel. Yet, bottom-of-the-funnel content can be extremely profitable given its direct relationship with sales. Even if search volumes may be low, be sure to target a sufficient amount of content at the bottom-of-the-funnel.
- In today's SEO landscape, you should be using AI-based optimization tools to plan your content and to ensure your content is thoroughly optimized for higher Google rankings.
- An effective strategy for achieving greater marketing ROI is to dominate the page in Google for your most important keywords. This means using multiple assets to help you occupy more real estate in the Google search results page.

- To improve your content performance, prune old content prior to creating new content. Make sure you're working from a solid foundation first.
- Get more ROI out of your content by repurposing it into different formats, shapes, and sizes. Remember it's not about merely copying and pasting from the source content. It's about adapting your content based on the context.
- When you publish a new content piece, you're not done. Content distribution is just as important as content creation.
- To achieve maximum ROI from your content, treat it as a portfolio. It's not only about creating optimized content for Google. Produce content for PR, thought leadership, sales enablement, inbound link attraction, etc. as well.

4

ACCOUNT-BASED MARKETING

You want Accenture as a client?

Or perhaps IBM?

Or Capgemini?

If you know who you want to secure as your next clients, then you're going to love this chapter!

With account-based marketing (ABM), you're targeting specific B2B accounts, companies, or roles. The marketing material you produce will be personalized to those targets. The idea with account-based marketing is to target a select list of ideal accounts, and when possible to do so in a personalized manner. It's most effective when you are selling a high-priced product or service.

Many marketers claim that ABM delivers a higher ROI than any other form of B2B marketing. With this in mind, account-based marketing is an essential part of a modern lead generation strategy.

ABM is currently one of the strongest ways for a B2B company to increase marketing and lead gen performance. Seventy-six percent (76 percent) of respondents to an ITSMA and ABM Leadership Alliance Benchmark Study said that ABM outperforms every other marketing investment. The study further found that nearly half (45 percent) of respondents achieve double the ROI from ABM as their other marketing initiatives.[22] A 2021 Demandbase study found that the average annual contract value for ABM deals is 33 percent higher than non-ABM deals.[23]

For mature ABM programs, the results are off-the-charts amazing. According to the Terminus *State of ABM 2020* study, 79 percent of new opportunities for companies with mature ABM programs come from ABM. And these opportunities are high quality — the study found that 73 percent of overall revenue for these companies was a result of the ABM program.[24]

According to ITSMA, "Account-Based Marketing delivers the highest return on investment of any strategic B2B marketing approach. Period."[25]

As you can see, ABM should clearly be a key strategy for many B2B marketers.

Yet, as an agency, we continually encounter prospects that don't engage in ABM, and never have. I would venture to say that roughly 80 percent of the prospective B2B clients we meet have no experience with ABM.

How can this be?

How can an approach that delivers higher ROI than other forms of marketing be ignored by so many marketing teams?

Looks like a prime opportunity to rethink lead generation!

How ABM Works

There are several types of ABM, including strategic ABM, ABM lite, and programmatic ABM. Strategic ABM and ABM lite is what I cover in this chapter, as I feel they are more powerful and effective. They are both based on customization to an ideal set of target accounts. Strategic ABM involves customization on an account or more granular level, while ABM lite is a one-to-few approach in which you target a number of accounts that have similar pain points or needs.

Programmatic ABM, on the other hand, is what just about every ABM software company offers. It's a scalable approach to targeted advertising, and often, personalization of web pages. Although it's more scalable in terms of the potential individuals you can reach, customization per account can be limited. In this way, it's a good way to target relevant audiences, but in my opinion it's limited in its effectiveness. It can often lack the customization required to resonate more deeply with the target accounts.

With strategic ABM, the first step in developing a successful program is to identify the accounts that you would value most as clients. Then, once you have that list, you research and define the specific individuals within each account whom you will target and strive to build relationships with. You then engage in ongoing, targeted outreach to such individuals, fully customized to what you feel would be the most relevant communications and messaging for each account and individual.

Ideally, over time, you begin to engage and to build a relationship with these individuals. If you're targeting correctly, you're reaching out to those whom your brand can help the most, and so it's an activity centered on helping others.

ABM is not limited, though, to cold outreach. You're likely to use pre-existing relationships and networks to help you communicate with decision-makers at your target companies where you can.

Keep in mind that you don't need to limit your ABM efforts to non-clients either. Among your larger clients, there may be other divisions, other departments, other offices, and other groups that are in need of your services and represent just as much a new sales opportunity as any non-client company.

ABM vs. Inbound Marketing

With inbound marketing, it's more of a "quantity over quality" game.

The goal with inbound is to generate a lot of leads and follow-up with them in order to qualify as many as possible. Gradually, you filter those leads down to a few prospects who are willing, able, and interested in buying, and you focus on those. But it's understood that the majority may not be highly qualified.

Think of ABM as the exact opposite. It's essentially flipping the funnel on its head. You start with your ideal prospects. You leapfrog the top of the funnel and jump right into outreach and engagement that, often with inbound marketing, would be reserved for the middle or lower of the funnel.

Whereas with inbound marketing, you never know who may contact you until they do, with ABM you know exactly who you'll target and the exact brand touchpoints they will have.

Both ABM and inbound marketing serve a purpose, and I encourage you to use both. But they are exact opposites.

The Magic Question

As an agency, our team at Stratabeat talks with many prospective clients. As part of this process, we have the opportunity to ask many marketing teams to name their top 100 target accounts. In other words, if they could wave a magic wand, which companies would they have as clients next.

This is a rather basic question. After all, if you don't know which companies would be your ideal clients, then who in the world is supposed to know?

Often, the answers come back vague and without conviction. After a few obvious names, our question is typically met with silence.

So, ask your own marketing team. Can you name the top 100 companies that you would most like to have as your next clients? If you can't, how about the top 50? Top 25? If you cannot name 25 at the very least, it's time to start analyzing your market in more detail, and to start exploring ABM as a new addition to your lead generation mix. This would be low-hanging fruit for massive lead generation improvement.

Creating $500,000 Out Of Thin Air

Many video production companies hit a brick wall when COVID-19 caused businesses to stop all new video work. Some of them folded. Others slimmed down to skeleton teams to ride out the storm.

Ryan Reed is the President of Rewatchable, one of our agency's video production partners. When COVID-19 hit, he saw his business dry up overnight. "We died as a business during COVID," he confided.

Luckily, I had previously recommended ABM to Reed for building his video business. What ABM did for Reed and Rewatchable is nothing short of remarkable.

Here's his story:

Rewatchable was growing fast when COVID hit. October of 2019 was the firm's biggest revenue month to date as a company. They were excited. Everything was going great.

But then in November, all of their science company clients disappeared due to the impact from China. They got hit about three months before the U.S. did with the coronavirus.

Reed knew that the pandemic was going to have a devastating impact on his business. He sensed that they were going to be decimated. By April, he had significantly reduced his staff. And the future was looking bleak.

"So we kind of needed to swing for the fences," he explained. This meant launching an ABM campaign.

He told his team that if their largest client didn't come back, realistically they would have to become freelancers and he would just have to wait until companies were willing to create videos again.

"We invested a whole week of our time," Reed continued. "We made personalized videos for three companies that we knew were still doing business. They're billion dollar companies, but they weren't marketing at the time due to the pandemic. So, we made one video for our largest client, a leading provider of scientific lab equipment and supplies. And then we made a talking-head video for a financial forecasting software company and one for an enterprise software company."

The video for Rewatchable's largest client turned the business around in the span of three days!

Reed explained what he and his team did to save the business. "We made one of our 'otter videos', which has a cartoon otter as the moderator. During normal times we had been producing a science video series for the client. And that week we made a fake episode of the series, using the same lab background, in our office using two green screens where our team members were 20 feet apart. Meanwhile, it was narrated by a cartoon otter. And then we basically just laid it all out there. 'We miss you guys. We want to get working with you guys again. Anything we can do to get things rolling, please let us know.' We talked about our vaccines. We talked about everything that we were doing to make it so that we could work again safely.

"Then we sent the video off. It was terrifying because who knew what would happen. We didn't know what their situation was. We hadn't heard from them in months.

Reed continued, "Then, about six hours later the phone started ringing. At first, it was the weirdest thing. It was someone from a different group at the company that had seen the video. I was wondering how they knew about the video. We had sent the video to only the team that we had been working with, which was about four people.

"The person on the phone had received it from her marketing group director, who had received it from her marketing group director, who had received it from the boss of the people that we work with there. It was just getting passed around like crazy."

The Massachusetts client team was still so restricted that they couldn't even entertain the notion of continuing the science series. But because of that video, it woke up every other part of the client's business. So, every Zoom recording, every motion graphic-based video that they were making, every single internal video, they started throwing at Rewatchable. All from that single customized ABM video.

"We're now in parts of the company that we had never spoken with before."

After that success, Rewatchable sent off other customized ABM videos. One company was focused on mainframe modernization, with an aging core audience and workforce. COVID hit, and stakeholders and customers were literally getting sick and passing away. Tonally, the business was not in a position to market itself during COVID.

"A big part of our business with them was livestreaming town halls, stuff that just wasn't going to happen during the pandemic. So, I put together a personal video of me talking to the camera and saying, 'Hey, we miss you guys. If there's anything we can do…' And then I laid out five ideas for videos that they could still produce in COVID that would be effective without feeling tone-deaf."

Reed sent the personalized video, but heard nothing back. Several weeks passed without word from the company. And then he finally got a call from the CMO, "Hey, thank you for the video. I'm so sorry we haven't talked to you. You can tell we're not doing a lot of customer-facing marketing, but we are starting to do corporate messaging. We're doing a lot of internal video."

The company then started bringing Rewatchable in for those types of videos, which is something that they had not done with them before. Over the course of a year and a half, Rewatchable has been producing many different types of internal videos for the company. Another major ABM win.

The third personalized video that Rewatchable sent out was to a financial forecasting software company. It had been a consistent client, and so it stung for Rewatchable to lose that revenue.

Reed and his team made another talking head video, because the software company also had an older client base.

Rewatchable customized the message and voice for the company and proceeded to ship it out the door. Although they didn't receive a response for six months, they finally did hear from them: "We're doing our 2022 budgeting, and we loved the video that you sent. We wanted to get a price list and make sure that we included you in our budgeting for 2022."

Three for three! ABM was batting 1,000 percent for Reed and his team.

In a nutshell, that's how Rewatchable started doing ABM. The company was dead in the water, and then decided to go "all in" on ABM and everything turned around.

The result for Rewatchable was $500,000 in incremental revenue in the initial year from starting their ABM journey. What's truly remarkable about the story is that this source of revenue would have been literally zero had they not reached out and communicated in a personalized manner.

Enhancing the Quality Of New Leads

Another example of a company using ABM to achieve serious business results is ServiceNow, a digital workflow solutions company. The marketing team was eager for a way to achieve breakthrough lead gen results.

ServiceNow had historically relied on paid search and events for lead generation. The big question for the marketing team was whether it was delivering the right prospects to the sales team. This was the overwhelming challenge the team faced every day. Although the company was able to get a flood of leads through marketing vehicles such as content syndication, the problem was that they wouldn't convert. They just weren't qualified nor were they of high quality.

ServiceNow needed a vehicle to produce more qualified leads. It changed its strategy and targeted more than 750 accounts via ABM. As part of the effort, ServiceNow customized and optimized its website to better serve its target accounts.

The result? One hundred new clients within a year.

Combining IP Detection And ABM

Yet one more example of a company using ABM effectively is Leadfeeder, the IP detection software company mentioned earlier in the book, that helps you detect who is on your website. Leadfeeder shows how the combination of IP detection and ABM makes a potent lead generation formula.

Through IP detection and ABM, Leadfeeder was able to close the largest account in the company's history. Here's how they did it.

First, they defined their ideal customer profile (ICP), audience personas, and target ABM accounts.

The sales team then started reaching out to these accounts to start building relationships. In parallel, Leedfeeder configured alerts within the Leadfeeder software installed on the company's website so that the team would be notified when a target account was on the website. This enabled the sales team to be timely with their communications with those accounts. Once a target company was on the site, the team sprang into action, reaching out and engaging with individuals who matched their ICP. The activity included email, direct mail, social media, and phone.

Intent data that was being captured by their own software helped them to see what each account was interested in so that they could customize communications accordingly. Seeing each account's engagement level on the site helped the team to assess priority levels, and the high-priority accounts were then targeted by the marketing team on LinkedIn through ebooks gated by lead gen forms.[26]

Andy Culligan, Leadfeeder's CMO at the time, explained to me, "We have our total addressable market list already mapped out. And with that, what we've started to do is take the Leadfeeder data of anybody that's been visiting from specific companies to the site, extracting that information and then pulling it into LinkedIn to retarget them.

"So, we cross reference it back to our total addressable market list, which we have already uploaded into Leadfeeder. And then it's doing a match when one of those companies comes to the site from the total addressable market list. And then what we're able to do is then extract that information out to retarget them even further."

By targeting companies that they knew had an interest in Leadfeeder (as demonstrated by their site engagement), the company wound up closing the largest account in the organization's history through ABM.

ABM Is Still In Its Early Stages

Even though ABM has been around for a number of years, and even though companies deeply engaged in ABM are seeing outsized success as demonstrated in the examples above, ABM execution in the market is still in its infancy.

For those paying attention, this represents a significant opportunity. Those who make ABM a priority now can capitalize on this gap in the market.

The ITSMA and ABM Leadership Alliance study mentioned above found that 67 percent of the study's respondents were still in the "Exploring" or "Experimenting" phases of their ABM programs. Merely 13 percent responded that the ABM program had achieved "Embedded" status. Similarly, only 13 percent responded to the Terminus *State of ABM 2020* study that their sales and marketing teams were fully integrated into the ABM program.

What this means is that your competitors are likely not doing ABM or still in the early stages of trying it out. While they are dipping their toes in the water, it's an opportunity for you to go "all-in" and seize new accounts.

Be strategic. While they zig, you should zag. Make ABM a cornerstone of your lead generation and relationship-building efforts.

The Dream 100 (or 200 or 300)

Chet Holmes explains what he calls the "Dream 100" in his book *The Ultimate Sales Machine: Turbocharge Your Business with Relentless Focus on 12 Key Strategies*. It was essentially an early version of ABM. The process involves the identification of the top 100 accounts you'd like to work with the most, and then regularly making efforts to build a relationship with them.

Using this method, he doubled the ad sales of a Charlie Munger magazine three years in a row.

How?

Holmes uncovered that out of the magazine's database of 2,200 potential advertisers, only 167 companies were responsible for 95 percent of the advertising in the top four magazines in the market. However, none of these firms was advertising with Munger's magazine...yet.

So, Holmes started reaching out to these advertisers every single month. Within a year, he secured 30 of them, doubling the magazine's ad sales. By the end of the third year, all 167 companies were buying ads in the magazine.

In another instance of the Dream 100 at work, Holmes was hired by an office equipment company. Previously, the company had distributed a direct mail piece to 20,000 potential buyers. The response? A big fat donut. Nada. Zero.

Holmes reviewed the company's sales, sifting through deals ranging from $10,000 to $28,000. Then, he noticed one sale for $160,000 and asked about it. He was told it was a sale to a big company.

Holmes then decided that the office equipment firm would target only large companies.

They identified 2,000 prospective large companies to target. In order to identify the most promising among them, he had his client's sales reps contact every single one of them. When on the phone, they explained that they were taking an industry survey, and asked just two questions:

- Can you tell us what type of computer system you have?
- How old is it?

More than 99 percent of the receptionists with whom they spoke answered the questions. Through their efforts, they were able to identify which companies were most likely spending more on maintenance than they would on a lease for a brand-new system.

In just two days, Holmes and the sales reps identified their "Dream 508" list with computer systems of at least five years old.

An all-out outreach effort ensued, and sales went through the roof.

Whether it's a Dream 100, Dream 200, Dream 508, or Dream 1,000 list, identifying your top prospects and then focusing your outreach on them like a laser works. The only thing surprising about it is that more companies are not doing it.

Getting Creative

Beyond targeting the right accounts, rethink your approach to ABM. Get creative. Break the mold.

Anyone can target verticals. Anyone can target accounts. But can you break through the noise, grab their attention, captivate them, and ultimately deliver overwhelming value?

Even with ABM, it pays to rethink what you're doing and how you're doing it in order to ensure greater success.

Our team at Stratabeat loves the concept of customization at scale. Yes, we're conducting outreach to many target accounts multiple times monthly. But that doesn't prevent us from being continually creative with our efforts.

For certain ABM campaigns, for example, we'll launch 50 or 100 custom knowledge hubs on the same day for a client. Each of the knowledge hubs is customized for one of the client's respective target accounts. It's this type of all-out blitz that helps them achieve a level of customization that their competitors can only dream about. And that's the type of creativity that generates results.

The creativity in ABM can take many forms. For example, for one client, we created giant four-foot by three-foot movie tickets and mailed them to hundreds of high-priority prospects. The recipients at each target account received a ticket with a customized URL on the front, taking them to a custom landing page. On the page they would find a customized message, along with a fully custom video just for the given account, filled with unique insight applicable to only that account.

For others, we created a podcast in which we solicited our client's target accounts to appear as featured guests. This program has sometimes been so strong that the majority of guests go on to become qualified leads engaged with the sales team.

Ask 100 marketers what an ABM campaign looks like, and the vast majority would never say it looks like this. But that's why it's so important to rethink common practices and to come up with something better. Because you'll achieve stronger results.

As you can see, the type of creativity that tends to work effectively delivers value for the target account. It's not about being internally focused and trying to sell your products or technology. It's about being focused on delivering value.

Creating A Dream Event

Speaking of creativity in ABM, just wait until you hear what Heidi Bullock did in generating outsized ROI for Engagio, prior to its acquisition by Demandbase.

Engagio provided an ABM automation platform for B2B marketers. Bullock, CMO at Engagio at the time (she has since moved on to become the CMO at the customer data solutions company Tealium), walked me through how she used ABM at Engagio to generate high ROI from events like Dreamforce, an annual Salesforce event that has over 170K registered attendees based in San Francisco.

For most events, marketers scan leads at the booth. Bullock wanted to break through all the noise, and so her team went in the opposite direction with their approach.

Specifically, they established a standalone venue called the "Engagio Open House" for meetings during the conference, hosted a big party at the Museum of Modern Art (MoMA), and also participated in a partner's lounge.

"The first part of our plan was to invite our target accounts with a combination of personalized emails and direct mail," Bullock pointed out. At the time, Engagio had three tiers of target accounts and the direct mail varied from a high-end whiskey to a postcard with 3-D glasses. "Tier one accounts received whiskey and were invited to a VIP party at the MoMA. Tier two and three accounts were invited to the main party. We also involved partners to increase our reach and marketing. We would agree on the accounts ahead of time to invite to ensure the focus was there and companies were not getting multiple versions of invitations. We were able to secure meetings with key accounts ahead of the event, which was great."

Bullock continued, "The second part of our plan was to actively market our programs onsite at Dreamforce. We invited prospects and customers to our 'Open House' venue, the MoMA party, and our content sessions at the partner lounge.

"Lastly, we were very thoughtful about an ongoing follow-up plan. This included different communications for customers and our target accounts. We did not just stop after the first follow-up. We continued to evaluate the program and tried different strategies to ensure we would hit our goals. That is a key success factor. Many folks you engage with may not respond to a follow-up email or call, but you should give it some time and try again."

How did ABM fare for Bullock and her team?

Really, it's nothing short of "Holy Cow" amazing!

They set up 30 meetings ahead of Dreamforce and 105 meetings during the event, for a combined total of 135 meetings from the ABM effort. This resulted in more than $2.3 million in pipeline within two months following the event.

Think about what 135 meetings with high-priority prospects would do for your business!

The key, according to Bullock, was taking advantage of an event where many of their key prospects and customers would be. By personalizing invitations and having unique activities, the goal was to make people feel extra special. In addition, the post-event focus was relentless, with a tailored and highly personalized message versus a standard nurture track.

So, as you can see, creativity can be applied in many different ways to ABM. The more creative you are, the more you can cut through all the clutter, captivate your target accounts, and achieve high ROI.

Closing The Loop With A Customized Website Experience

Once you've captured the attention of your target accounts through ABM, how do you ensure a better experience for them?

In talking with Dave Gerhardt, former Chief Brand Officer (and VP of Marketing prior to that) at Drift, introduced earlier in the book, he explained that you can use conversational marketing in your website to close the loop on ABM efforts for far greater impact. He spoke of a time that he received an ABM package that must have cost $70 or $80. He then went to the website, and it was a completely generic experience. There was literally nothing customized for his visit.

It was a lost opportunity for the company to add value or to further differentiate themselves.

Gerhardt pointed out that you do ABM precisely to target your best target accounts. So, why in the world wouldn't you customize the experience?

With his company's chatbot solution, they can recognize ABM accounts and can continue the campaign as the relevant people reach the website. By using targeted messaging and chatbots to engage with leads in real-time while they are still on your website, you're creating a more seamless, personalized experience that will lead to a higher conversion rate.

"Why not greet your target accounts," Gerhardt continued, "with a personalized message from the sales rep, and they can skip the line? They don't have to fill out a form, they don't have to wait. They can send you a message, and that sales rep can be on the golf course or walking to Starbucks and they get a notification on their phone that hey, Tom is on your website right now, do you want to chat with him? And so it really provides an amazing personalized one-to-one experience for all your target accounts that visit your website."

Expanding Existing Accounts

ABM is highly effective for starting new relationships and acquiring new customers. It's equally effective at helping to expand reach within existing accounts, as was seen above with Rewatchable's use of ABM.

When Adi Reske was Industry Marketing Director, Financial Services, at Pegasystems, she and her team used ABM to expand within accounts. For example, after they won the JPMorgan Chase account, they turned around and sold the same system to JPMorgan Chase Retail, then another division, and then yet another division, etc.

In other words, once they secured an initial foothold, they radiated from that point across the enterprise.

That was the core strategy of her team, and ABM needed to support it for the approach to work effectively. What Reske and her team did with JPMorgan Chase was to create a community of JPMorgan Chasers. One aspect of this, for example, was to conduct a monthly internal webinar exclusively for those at JPMorgan Chase. They invited the people that they knew — clients and prospects, but also people that were completely new to Pegasystems.

And a brilliant twist on ABM in Pegasystems' case was that they orchestrated presentations during these webinars by champions at JPMorgan Chase to others at the corporation. The presentations were typically about initiatives they had implemented using Pegasystems software and how it helped them. In other words, they got the JPMorgan Chase employees to sell to other employees.

The conversion rate was sky high. ROI was off the charts. The only cost was their time.

Another example of community-building by Reske and her team was an account-specific LinkedIn group that they created and managed. It was of benefit to those at JPMorgan Chase, as they were able to connect and network with others within the enterprise.

Once a year, Pegasystems would have its annual customer event, so her team would create mini events just for those in the LinkedIn group. On the first day of an event, they would facilitate introductions among the JPMorgan Chasers, helping them to build relationships inside their own organization. The group reacted very positively, and the momentum then further enhanced other interactions between Pegasystems and JPMorgan Chase.

According to Reske, "I think that with account-based marketing, if you're doing it right, ROI and conversion rates are the best."

Assessing Accounts Holistically

As you can see, ABM is an effective approach for both connecting with new accounts as well as expanding within existing accounts. In addition, it's a way for you to understand accounts more holistically.

Look at WP Engine as an example of this. When Mary Ellen Dugan was CMO at the company, she explained to me, "Our demand generation is based on a culture of innovation, which can take on various forms. For example, we are pushing the boundaries on our technology stack, which speaks to our focus on innovation. Account-based marketing isn't new, but we approach it with a focus on collaboration by orchestrating the data across platforms for a holistic view of the account. Our efforts are triangulated like a heat map based on signals and intent versus simply implementing ABM. We lean heavily on great content and captivating creative to engage with our prospects."

In looking back at the history of ABM at WP Engine, the company has experimented with different software packages and on top of that has conducted split testing within ABM initiatives to assess what resonates the most.

Different data points. Different angles. Different insights.

Use ABM to attain a deeper level of understanding of each target account.

Why You Should Add Account-Based Marketing To Your Lead Generation Strategy

ABM facilitates the integration of sales and marketing teams. In a traditional siloed system, marketing develops the leads, then hands them off to sales to close the deal. With ABM, sales and marketing work collaboratively to identify accounts, generate leads, and find solutions that work for each account. ABM encourages all departments to work together, even the C-Suite, product development, and customer service.

ABM helps you drive greater revenue. ABM leads to higher close rates and larger average deal sizes. As mentioned earlier, a 2021 Demandbase study found that the average annual contract value for ABM deals is 33 percent higher than non-ABM deals. This makes sense. By focusing on targeted, high-value accounts, you immediately gain a strategic advantage in the sales process.

While ABM may require more time to process fewer leads, the difference in conversion rate and deal size makes it more likely you'll see greater revenue and higher ROI.

In addition, ABM Is extremely effective for high-ticket Items. If you sell products or services with a long sales cycle and high price tags, ABM can be more efficient at helping you to connect with and nurture high-quality accounts who fully appreciate your value. Inbound marketing, in comparison, may result in many inquiries from those who could never make a purchase at your price point (or for a variety of other reasons), wasting your team's time and diverting your resources from those who matter most to your business. For high-ticket items, it's far more effective to be hyper-targeted, and ABM enables you to do that.

How To Absolutely Crush It With ABM

Deliver as much value as possible with every touchpoint. In your ABM outreach, you should never be conducting outreach simply for the sake of conducting outreach. Instead, provide as much value as you can with each brand touchpoint.

- What custom analysis can you be providing?
- What can you teach them that they do not already know?
- What would they find useful?
- How can you arm them with new insight?
- How can you help them make more money?
- How can you help them achieve greater efficiency or save money?

- How can you better prepare them for the future of their industry?

Also, personalize your outreach. Targeting ideal accounts via ABM doesn't mean you need to target only one audience in your campaigns. For example, you can target specific industries, accounts, departments, roles, and/or individuals. You can create templated content pieces with some customization, or customize your content for each and every account. When you get to know specific individuals, personalize your communications accordingly.

The more you can customize your content for the intended recipients, the more success you'll likely achieve with your ABM program. The higher the ticket item, the more important personalization becomes.

Jessica Rathke, Principal at FluentSales, points out that personalization needs to factor not only the person, but their location and environment. "Our messages must resonate with the people we are communicating with. Personalization takes on a whole new dimension when we include international markets into the mix. Language, culture, and other factors become crucial."

This is an important point that is sometimes overlooked. If your client is in a different country or if the account is global and you're dealing with individuals in different regions, be sensitive to the cultural differences. When I worked in Japan, I saw this occasionally with those outside of the country trying to do business with Japanese companies. It's critical to understand as much as possible about the people and culture, or your success may be frustratingly limited.

Beyond personalization, be relentlessly consistent with your ABM program to better ensure success. When you conduct your ABM program, develop a calendar and ensure that you are consistently creating brand touchpoints. You don't want to send four emails and a direct mailer to an account in one month, conduct no correspondence the following month, follow that up with one phone call the subsequent month, and then hit them with four emails, three LinkedIn messages, and an executive briefing the next month.

Be consistent.

Define the ideal number of brand touchpoints you'll create, and then stick to that plan. If you think you need to engage on a weekly basis, then follow through. If you think bi-weekly makes more sense, fine. If you think monthly works better for your audience, then monthly it is.

The point is, don't overwhelm them at any time, and don't go a long period of time without contact either. As long as you are adding value with each touchpoint, then keeping in front of them consistently is what's important. When they are ready to engage, they will.

—

Along with consistency, be opportunistic with your ABM program. When you conduct your ABM campaigns, keep track of who is on your website and what they are doing there. Sometimes the recipients of your emails, LinkedIn messages, or direct mail pieces go to your website without clicking a link or typing in a custom URL. Or, they may request someone else on their team to check out your website and see what you're all about.

In any and every instance, if they are visiting your website, you want to know.

And it's not just their visits that you want to record. You want to know every page they visited, the time on each page, and the navigational flow of the visit.

So, as was outlined in the Leadfeeder example above, use IP detection software to identify the target companies visiting your site, whether part of a specific outreach campaign or not. IP detection software helps you understand how they got to your site, when they were on your site, and exactly which pages they visited (with the time-on-page information to boot). By using custom filters in your software, you can quickly identify qualified site visitors demonstrating the right intent so that you can be highly opportunistic in reaching out to them.

—

With ABM, you're likely targeting hundreds of accounts. The only way to effectively do this is if the program is built to scale. Trying to do everything manually or as one-off efforts is inefficient and unscalable.

There are various CRM, marketing automation, and ABM-specific software solutions that help you to achieve more with less effort. Or, you can use a custom database solution. The point is, use technology to help you scale your program.

And on the implementation side, consider the value of adding customization or personalization on top of templated materials to help you scale your efforts wherever possible. For example, if you're creating a video as part of your ABM program, customize the initial 20 percent or 30 percent, but then include templated content for the remainder.

Use repeatable templates so that you can launch web pages quickly and easily.

Another implementation strategy is to first target at the vertical level, and then go more granular with only those specific accounts you see actually visiting your website or engaging with your content. In this way, you're enabling them to self qualify themselves.

Alerts are another way to add automation to your ABM mix in enhancing scalability. Set up automated alerts for when your target accounts are on your website. In addition, configure alerts for any type of company news (Google Alerts is easy to set up for this purpose.), enabling you to capture new insight more readily and to follow up accordingly with those accounts in a timely manner.

Chapter Summary

Account-based marketing is all about defining your ideal clients and then actively targeting accounts as part of an overall outreach and customization regimen. For many marketing teams, ABM delivers a higher ROI than any other form of B2B marketing. With this in mind, ABM is an essential part of a modern lead generation strategy.

- ABM is one of the strongest ways for a B2B company to increase marketing performance.
- ABM helps your organization to increase revenue, as well as your average deal size. ABM is especially productive for high-ticket items.
- ABM can help you to connect and build relationships with new accounts, or to expand within existing

accounts. It also helps you to understand accounts more holistically.
- The first step with ABM is to identify the accounts that you would value most as clients. Ideally, these are the companies that you can help the most.
- Once you have your ABM target account list, research the specific individuals within each account who match your ideal customer profile. Strive to build relationships with them.
- Engage consistently in ongoing, targeted outreach.
- Customize and personalize your outreach, and provide as much value with each touchpoint as possible.
- Be creative! Whether you're creating giant-sized movie tickets tied to custom landing pages or launching 100 account-specific knowledge hubs on the same day, use your imagination to leave your competition in the dust.
- To achieve the strongest ABM results, marketing and sales should work together.

5

REFERRALS

Generating leads through referrals is invaluable for any B2B business. An estimated 84 percent of B2B decision makers start the buying process directly from a referral, while peer recommendations influence more than 90 percent of B2B buying decisions overall.[27]

Leads that are sourced from referrals tend to be highly qualified and are typically the highest-converting leads. In fact, B2B referrals deliver a 70 percent higher conversion rate than other types of leads.[27] Not only do they tend to convert at a higher rate, but they also tend to be more loyal and more profitable.

Luckily, people are naturally wired to connect and share information with others. It's just part of human nature. Individuals enjoy being part of a tribe, and as such, they enjoy helping others. On the flip side, when they make a referral, they gain social credibility as having insider information or simply as being a valuable resource. So, a referral benefits the referrer in multiple ways.

When thinking of B2B lead generation, referrals are typically among the most promising. This is because they are coming at you warmer than many other types of leads. They trust the referrer, and so you're leapfrogging a major hurdle in the sales process. By receiving a vote of confidence (sometimes an effusive vote) from a trusted source, you enjoy the strongest kind of social proof just before you talk with the prospect.

Looking at our own agency, one of the strongest and most consistent lead sources for Stratabeat is referrals. We receive referrals from not only existing clients, but also past clients, partners, contractors, and others in our network.

Generating leads through referrals is common for many agencies. However, where most companies get referrals wrong is that they leave them completely to chance. They never actively focus on maximizing referral-sourced leads, but instead just passively await random referrals that may or may not come their way. The surprising reality is that only 30 percent of B2B companies have a formal referral program in place.[28] This is just nuts!

Instead, it's time to rethink referrals!

Just as your marketing team plans for a new website or develops a content calendar, referrals should be treated as a program to be actively managed. Through my many years in marketing, I've seen groups get together for meetings on practically everything. Brand strategy? Check. New website updates? Check. Content strategy? Check? SEO? Check? Quarterly and weekly plans? Check.

Referrals? Uh, nope.

Why is that? Why are referrals treated as a low priority? As an afterthought? As something that should be random? It just doesn't add up, yet it's the reality for many B2B companies.

Build A Referral Program

Instead of leaving referrals to chance, build a documented referral development program. Too many companies take a random approach, passively waiting for referrals to come in the door. Instead, be proactive in nurturing your network.

Ask for referrals as a standard practice.

Determine the frequency with which you'll conduct outreach, or the triggers that will dictate the timing of your referral requests. Determine how you'll reach out. And be sure to figure out how you'll offer value to these individuals.

Include your referral program in your annual and quarterly marketing plans, and then track your performance and adjust as needed.

Why is all this important?

Well, it all comes down to trust. Who do they trust the most? One of the critical factors in any sale is whether or not they trust you. Are you going to help them solve their problems? Are you going to help them achieve their goals? When trying to choose among multiple options, trust is a major ingredient in their final decision.

Referral marketing is a rocketship to achieving trust. There's little else in marketing that helps you to make such a strong impression so quickly on a brand new lead.

The bottom line is, build more trust, and you'll close more deals. A structured referral development program helps you successfully build a moat of trust around your business — something that positions you with an immediate advantage over competitors.

Establish The Triggers

Establish the triggers for when you'll ask for a referral. For example, you may want to reach out to your network based on a calendar, such as once a quarter or twice a year.

In addition to an outreach calendar, establish standard triggers at your company for asking for referrals. This may be when a client contract has just renewed, for instance. Or, it may be after a major win for your client. You do not necessarily need to wait until after a project has been completed. If you've proven your worth, expertise, and value, they will likely be happy to start sending referrals your way.

The important thing to remember is to make your referral program an ongoing endeavor. Too many companies that rely on referrals don't follow up with customers or others in their network. Make sure you're defining various triggers for your team to reach out, and try to ensure you'll be creating multiple touch points throughout the year.

Identify Your Network For Referrals

Define your network for referrals. This could be clients. Might be past clients. This could also be partners and any other colleagues or associates. Could even be someone on LinkedIn who is connected to those you wish to work with or is simply someone you admire and respect.

What's important is that you place these individuals into their respective groups, and document everything. Keep track of your communications, and make sure that you're reaching out to the individuals in each group multiple times a year.

Prioritize

Who are your best clients? Who are the ones who would sing your praises to the high heavens? The ones who gain tremendous value from what you do for them? The ones who make you blush with their effusive praise?

Start with them.

With referrals, it's important to prioritize. You don't necessarily need to seek referrals from all clients, but it is critical that you're tapping your best clients, who are going to act as a powerful extended sales force for you.

What could be stronger in lead gen? (Very little.)

Different organizations and different individuals can introduce you to different types of prospective clients.

Some clients are VIPs. Others may not be.

The same is true with referral sources. They are all highly valued. They are all amazing. But some are going to be VIPs and others are not. It's your job to prioritize the VIPs and go out of your way to assist and support them. Shower them with value. Spend time building the relationship.

Make It Personal

You can occasionally include a generic request for referrals in your email marketing or direct mail. But what's 100X better is to make your requests personal. Customize them for each person and each request.

If there's something that relates to a specific conversation you had with them, point it out. If something ties to a personal aspiration of theirs, make note of it and try to help them achieve their goals. If you notice that they achieved something special, or that their company made an important announcement, send a note of congratulations.

Making your communications personal is not as scalable as just blasting out the same message to everyone in your network. However, it's worth it. With a personalized approach, you'll ultimately achieve a far higher ROI.

Remember, your network is full of real people. No one wants to feel like a number. They want to feel recognized and appreciated, as they deserve to be. Take the time to personalize your outreach for each individual.

Provide Value

If you find something useful online, why not share it with those in your network? It could be an interesting article. Or a fascinating video. Or something simply new and useful, like a new Google feature.

What's probably most valuable is information that will help their company make more money, or perhaps information that helps the individual save time or advance in their career.

What's going to be helpful to one person may be irrelevant to another, though. So again, it comes back to making it personal. Think about their industry, their role, and their specific goals and challenges. Then do your outreach only when you think there's value in it for them.

For example, let's say someone in your network loves Japan. You can reach out with any interesting or intriguing news coming out of the island nation. Or you can take them to a Japanese restaurant for lunch. You get the point.

Frame The Benefits

What I don't advise is simply reaching out to a group of people and asking for referrals. If you do this too many times, you're going to annoy a number of folks and piss off the others.

Remember, it's a relationship. It's not about you. It's about *both of you*.

Always try to think of them first. What's in it for them? What are the benefits to them?

For example, Stratabeat partners with a number of complementary agencies, where we don't offer the services of our partner and they don't offer our services. It's a clear win-win, as we're able to take care of a need of one of their clients, while in other cases they're able to address the need of one of our clients. Looking at it holistically, they win, their clients win, our clients win, and we win, as well.

Be Specific

When asking for a referral, don't ask, "Do you know anyone who could use our services?" Be more specific. This helps them think of people in their network, who may have highly defined needs.

For example, "Do you know a SaaS company that needs better SEO results?" or "Do you know any financial advisors that could use a new WordPress website?" or "Do you know any B2B green tech companies that are looking to generate more leads?", etc.

The more specific you are, the easier it will be for them to think of relevant individuals and companies for you.

Make It Easy For Others

Speaking of making it easier for them, tell them who your ideal clients would be. This helps them narrow in on those most qualified, while saving you from spending time on unqualified leads or those who would simply never be a fit.

If they have any questions, be extremely responsive. If they need any supporting materials, get it to them fast. Make it ridiculously easy for them to send you referrals.

Be Active On LinkedIn

Invest time on LinkedIn not only engaging with your network, but also exploring your network's potential connections. Look for networking opportunities. If you spot someone in their network whom you're eager to connect with, see if you can add any value to their relationship or for their connection specifically.

Be seen in LinkedIn. When you're posting, highlight the achievements of others. Mention something someone told you that made an impact on your life or career. Call it out when they do something impressive. Congratulate them on their wins. When appropriate, comment on others' posts and engage in conversations. Add value. Look to give. Help others look good.

Always think of it from the perspective of what's in it for them. Then, providing you with new referrals becomes much easier for others. But even without the referrals, I would strongly argue that you should be focused entirely on benefits to them.

It's all about them.

Offer A Rewards Program

For certain businesses, it may be appropriate to offer a structured rewards program. If your business tends to involve a lot of repeat purchases, this can be a highly effective way to get your customers acting as your sales force in recruiting new prospects.

But instead of offering something that might be perceived as a bribe (no matter how you intend it), consider offering complimentary products/services or a bonus service or a discount off of future services. When it's directly tied to your products or services, there's a relevancy factor where everyone wins.

Offer Unique Content

An effective way to organically grow your referrals is through the development of unique content. Offer high-quality content that they will value, and it's sure to be shared online, putting you in front of new prospective leads. Although not a direct referral, it serves as an indirect one.

Offer a special whitepaper, private Q&A, or executive briefing. Conduct proprietary research and turn the findings into a variety of content pieces. Offer a series of useful videos, webinars, or courses, etc.

Become a content marketing machine, and keep getting the word out there. As long as your content is amazing, you'll most likely wind up with many more leads.

Make Referrals To Others

Ironically, one of the most effective ways to increase your incoming referrals is to refer companies to clients, partners, and others in your network. Focus on helping them be successful. Make that the top priority.

If you get in the habit of making introductions yourself, those around you will naturally start to think of introductions for you, as well. It ultimately comes back to you in spades.

Get More ROI Out Of Your Email Signature

Your email signature is prime real estate to get your message out to your network. It can be a subtle way to remind others that they can refer others in need of services to you.

A beneficial aspect of using your email signature for lead generation is that you're emailing all day anyway and so it won't take up any more of your time. Just make sure your lead gen message is built into your email signature template. And better yet, use multiple email sig templates. That way, you can customize the message depending on the recipient.

Exceed Expectations

This one is easy. With whatever you do for your clients, always exceed expectations. Do this, and you'll definitely get more referrals.

Provide Ridiculous Levels Of Customer Service And Support

When your customers have questions or concerns, how prompt and thorough are you in taking care of them? Always strive to deliver the utmost in service and support. Make them feel important. Make them feel loved.

Most people tend to be reasonable. If a question arises with your products or services, that's natural. The important thing is how you react and ensure everything gets resolved to their satisfaction.

Case Studies And Testimonials

Even without a direct referral, your clients can help you by participating in case studies and/or providing you with a testimonial. These are technically not "referrals" per se, but they help others feel more comfortable giving you referrals. In addition, they help you increase your leads by acting as social proof and by acting as a client endorsement.

An effective way to secure new case studies and testimonials is to seek customer feedback first. If they tell you that everything is going great, then make your move by getting permission for a case study and securing a testimonial. (In the case that things are not so great, then it's an opportunity to see how to help them more effectively.) When receiving a new testimonial, see if they can highlight something unique about your solutions. This is a way to make your testimonials stronger.

Promote Social Sharing

As mentioned, be consistently generating new content that can easily be shared with others.

Then, make sure that your content is easily shared online. For example, offer captivating visuals. In blog posts, offer social sharing links. With an infographic, offer an HTML code snippet that can be easily dropped into their web page. However you can make it easier for them to share with others, you'll end up with more leads knocking at your door.

Partnerships

Again, even without a direct referral, you can leverage partnerships to get in front of new audiences with an implied endorsement.

For example, I'm often the featured guest on a number of webinars and podcasts. I've appeared on a number of webinars produced by the WordPress hosting platform WP Engine, presenting on topics ranging from SEO to lead generation to behavioral intelligence. WP Engine currently has more than 150,000 customers. By joining their webinars and presenting useful information to their audience, I get in front of a wide range of new prospects with each webinar, with the implied endorsement of a trusted company.

Not only that, but then the webinar recordings live on in WP Engine's website for years to come. This means the benefits of one webinar carry forward over several years.

So, although it's not a written testimonial per se, being featured on webinars and podcasts is one heck of an implied endorsement that carries the weight of multiple testimonials.

Survey Your Customers

Something you may want to experiment with is customer surveys. At the end of the survey, try asking for a testimonial or a referral. You may be surprised to see that some of your customers are very happy to provide you with one or both of these.

Capitalize on Positive Feedback

If a client tells you how ridiculously awesome your team is, capitalize on the opportunity by asking if they know of anyone who could benefit from the same products or services.

By engaging with them at a time when they are over the moon about your company, you increase the likelihood that they will offer up a few names.

Create a Community

Something that requires more work (much more work), but can be highly effective in building referral leads, is to build a community. If you center your community on your area of solutions or benefits, you'll be organically spreading the word about your brand. And the best part about it is that you'll be nurturing an army of potential referrers. As the host of a community, you naturally gain a certain level of status, respect, and trust. A community helps you accelerate your referral leads growth.

Follow Up

When someone sends you a new referral, thank them immediately. But then also remember to follow up, give them an update, and let them know how it works out.

Following up is one of the easiest tasks in the referral process, yet one of the most forgotten. Too often, referrals are made, and then the referring party never hears another word.

If you want ongoing referrals, you'll need to change your attitude. It's not a transaction. Referrals are part of a relationship. As such, the follow up is just as important as any other communication you have with your network.

Chapter Summary

Referrals tend to be some of the best leads. This is because they are coming at you warmer than many other types of leads. Referrals come with built-in trust, something that's invaluable for closing new business.

Too many companies, though, rely on referrals randomly. Instead, establish a program to ensure a continual flow of new leads.

- Establish a structured referral development program.
- Identity and nurture a referral network.
- Make your communications customized and personal. Try to avoid too many generic email blasts.
- Focus on providing value to your network. Always ask, "What's in it for them?"
- Be active on LinkedIn.
- Create unique content. Create content that can be easily

shared.
- Provide ridiculous levels of service and support. Make them happy!
- Capitalize on positive feedback. Make the request when they are extremely excited about what you've just done for them.
- Remember to follow up after receiving a referral. Thank them, give them updates, and let them know how it turns out. It's not a transaction; it's a relationship.

CONCLUSION

I hope that *Rethink Lead Generation* has helped you to uncover new opportunities and strategies to fuel your leads growth.

If your lead gen is essentially treading water, rethink what you're doing. Throw out the best practices. Use marketing jujitsu. Explore non-obvious ways to ignite leads growth.

When I wrote the book, I was focused on providing you with actionable methods for unleashing organic growth. To that end, the book outlines a range of ways to transform your website, SEO, content marketing, ABM, and referrals into a lead generation engine.

What I hope you walk away with is an overflowing river of new ideas for acquiring leads.

If you'd like to continue the journey of taking your lead generation to new heights, I invite you to join me over at TomShapiro.com for an ongoing flow of new information, posts, stories, and resources. Let's get you more leads!

NOTES

[1] *Masters of Scale*, https://mastersofscale.com/tristan-walker-beauty-of-a-bad-idea/

[2] Don Reisinger, "Why Tim Cook's Business Rule Is to Not Follow the Rules", *Inc.*, https://www.inc.com/don-reisinger/why-tim-cooks-business-rule-is-to-not-follow-rules.html

[3] Manda Mahoney, "The Subconscious Mind of the Consumer (And How To Reach It)", Working Knowledge, Harvard Business School, https://hbswk.hbs.edu/item/the-subconscious-mind-of-the-consumer-and-how-to-reach-it

[4] The Drift Marketing Team, *This Won't Scale*, Drift Press

[5] Josh Linkner, *Disciplined Dreaming: A Proven System to Drive Breakthrough Creativity*, Jossey-Bass, Page 2

[6] Brian Gregg, Jason Heller, Jesko Perrey, and Jenny Tsai, "The most perfect union: Unlocking the next wave of growth by unifying creativity and analytics", McKinsey & Company, https://www.mckinsey.com/business-functions/marketing-and-sales/our-insights/the-most-perfect-union

[7] Marc Brodherson, Jason Heller, Jesko Perrey, and David Remley, "Creativity's bottom line: How winning companies turn creativity into business value and growth", McKinsey & Company, https://www.mckinsey.com/business-functions/mckinsey-digital/our-insights/creativitys-bottom-line-how-winning-companies-turn-creativity-into-business-value-and-growth

[8] "The Creative Dividend: How Creativity Impacts Business Results", Forrester Consulting commissioned by Adobe, https://landing.adobe.com/dam/downloads/whitepapers/55563.en.creative-dividends.pdf

[9] "Enterprises That Emphasize Creativity Outperform Less Creative Counterparts", Tenovos, https://tenovos.com/the-creative-enterprise-survey/

[10] Ufuk Akcigit, John Grigsby, Tom Nicholas, "Immigration and the Rise of American Ingenuity", https://www.nber.org/system/files/working_papers/w23137/w23137.pdf

[11] Petra Moser, Alessandra Voena, Fabian Waldinger, "German Jewish Emigres and US Invention", *The American Economic Review*, https://www.jstor.org/stable/43495318?seq=1

[12] Alexandre N. Tuch, Eva E. Presslaber, Markus Stöcklin, Klaus Opwis, Javier A. Bargas-Avila, "The role of visual complexity and prototypicality regarding first impression of websites: Working towards understanding aesthetic judgments", https://static.googleusercontent.com/media/research.google.com/en/us/pubs/archive/38315.pdf

[13] "12th Annual Content Marketing Benchmarks, Budgets, and Trends: Insights for 2022", MarketingProfs and Content Marketing Institute commissioned by ON24, https://contentmarketinginstitute.com/wp-content/uploads/2021/10/B2B_2022_Research.pdf

[14] Tim Soulo, "How We Grew Traffic to Ahrefs' Blog by 1136% (and Got Thousands of Paying Customers)", https://medium.com/ahrefs-marketing/how-we-grew-traffic-to-ahrefs-blog-by-1136-and-got-thousands-of-paying-customers-1fbd7e6b145a

[15] "State of Original Research for Marketing 2019", BuzzSumo and Mantis Research, https://mantisresearch.com/wp-content/uploads/2019/08/State_of_Original_Research_2019.pdf

[16] "The State of Content Marketing 2020 Global Report", Semrush, https://www.semrush.com/state-of-content-marketing/

[17] "Ranking Factors, SEMrush Study 2.0", Semrush, https://www.semrush.com/ranking-factors/

[18] Katie Martell, "39 Essential Content Marketing Facts", Aberdeen, https://www.aberdeen.com/cmo-essentials/39-essential-content-marketing-facts/

[19] "Video Marketing Statistics 2021", Wyzowl, https://www.wyzowl.com/video-marketing-statistics/

[20] "Arrow Electronics Acquires United Technical Publishing", Mergr, https://mergr.com/arrow-electronics-acquires-united-technical-publishing

[21] "Arrow Electronics to Acquire EE Times for $23 Million", everythingRF, https://www.everythingrf.com/News/details/2601-arrow-electronics-to-acquire-ee-times-for-23-million

[22] "The ABM Leadership Alliance and ITSMA Release 2020 ABM Research Study", ITSMA, https://www.itsma.com/the-abm-leadership-alliance-and-itsma-release-2020-abm-research-study/

[23] "2021 ABM Benchmark Study", Demandbase, https://www.demandbase.com/ebook/2021-abm-benchmark-study-measurement/

[24] "Terminus 2020 State of ABM Report", Terminus, https://terminus.com/2020stateofabm/

[25] "Account-Based Marketing delivers the highest return on investment of any strategic B2B marketing approach. Period.", ITSMA, https://www.itsma.com/account-based-marketing-hot-topic/

[26] Jonny Butler, "How We Used Account-Based Marketing and Sales to Close Our Biggest Ever Deal", Leadfeeder, https://www.leadfeeder.com/blog/b2b-abm-marketing-sales/

[27] Laurence Minsky and Keith A. Quesenberry, "How B2B Sales Can Benefit from Social Selling", Harvard Business Review, https://hbr.org/2016/11/84-of-b2b-sales-start-with-a-referral-not-a-salesperson

[28] Jim Williams, "Infographic: 17 B2B Referral Statistics You Should Know (But Probably Don't)", Influitive, https://influitive.com/blog/infographic-17-stats-about-b2b-referrals-you-should-know-but-probably-dont/

ABOUT THE AUTHOR

TOM SHAPIRO is the Founder and CEO of Stratabeat, Inc., a B2B organic growth agency specializing in SEO, content development, content marketing, design, account-based marketing (ABM), and conversion optimization. Tom has developed marketing strategies for some of the world's leading companies, including Intel, GE, Hewlett-Packard, AT&T, and UnitedHealthcare. Previously, while Tom was Director of Digital Strategy at the marketing agency iProspect, the firm grew from 85 to more than 700 employees in a five-year period.

Tom is the author of *Rethink Lead Generation: Advanced Strategies to Generate More Leads for Your Business* and *Rethink Your Marketing: 7 Strategies to Unleash Revenue Growth.* His writings have appeared in Chief Marketer, CMO.com, CNN.com, Forbes, MarketingProfs, MediaPost, and many others.

To explore additional resources, visit:

TomShapiro.com

ABOUT RETHINK YOUR MARKETING

IF YOU'VE HIT A PLATEAU and your business is stuck, *Rethink Your Marketing: 7 Strategies to Unleash Revenue Growth* arms you with powerful strategies for growth. *Rethink Your Marketing* helps you to identify the specific levers of your marketing that will lead to new growth, enabling you to cut through the noise to what truly moves the needle.

Rethink Your Marketing includes marketing wisdom from more than 50 companies. Want to know how Russell Weiner, President at Domino's, created the fastest-growing restaurant in the U.S.? Want to know how Mark Organ took Eloqua from near bankruptcy to being acquired for $871 million? This book's got you covered!

Read *Rethink Your Marketing*, and learn to transform your business.

Learn more at:

RethinkYourMarketing.com

BOOK TOM TO SPEAK AT YOUR EVENT

MAKE YOUR NEXT EVENT EXCEPTIONAL with unique marketing insight. Tom Shapiro helps audiences to unleash growth through creative marketing strategies and lateral thinking.

Book Tom to speak, and enable your audience to learn how to:

- Generate more traffic, leads, and revenue.
- Apply neuroscience, psychology, and behavioral science to marketing for greater results.
- Increase SEO and content ROI.

Book Tom to speak at your next event:

TomShapiro.com/Speaking

ABOUT STRATABEAT

STRATABEAT, INC. is an organic growth agency for B2B companies. Services include search engine optimization (SEO), content development, content marketing, account-based marketing (ABM), design, and conversion optimization.

By injecting neuroscience, psychology, and behavioral science into your marketing, Stratabeat enables you to engage more deeply with your audience and to drive them to action. Generate significant results for your business through the combination of science and extreme creativity.

Learn more at:

Stratabeat.com

Made in the USA
Las Vegas, NV
07 January 2024